Please re
lates

A BOOK OF
SOUTH AFRICAN
VERSE

A BOOK OF
South African
Verse

SELECTED
AND INTRODUCED BY
GUY BUTLER

CAPE TOWN
OXFORD UNIVERSITY PRESS
TORONTO   LONDON

Oxford University Press, Ely House, London W.1
GLASGOW NEW YORK TORONTO MELBOURNE WELLINGTON
CAPE TOWN SALISBURY IBADAN NAIROBI LUSAKA ADDIS ABABA
BOMBAY CALCUTTA MADRAS KARACHI LAHORE DACCA
KUALA LUMPUR HONG KONG TOKYO
Oxford University Press, Thibault House, Cape Town

First published London 1959
Second impression Cape Town 1963
Third impression Cape Town 1968

PRINTED OFFSET BY
GOTHIC PRINTING COMPANY LTD
CAPE TOWN SOUTH AFRICA

To
ROY CAMPBELL
1901—1957

CONTENTS

ix

ACKNOWLEDGEMENTS and thanks are due to all the living poets, to publishers, and other copyright holders for permission to use the poems included in this anthology.

ACKNOWLEDGEMENTS

MARGARET ALLONBY for 'A Book for Christmas', *from* 'Lustration of the Winter Tree', 'O Theophilus', 'For Sheila', 'Eurydice' and 'Reflection'.

Mrs. H. R. Lake for 'The Poet', 'Seed', *from* 'The Luck in the Square Stone' and 'Recovery from Mental Illness' by H. C. BOSMAN.

W. R. G. BRANFORD for 'Trooper Temple Pulvermacher'.

N. H. BRETTELL for 'Elephant', 'Giraffes', 'Outside Kimberley', 'Cataclysm' and *from* 'Wind and an Eagle Owl' from *A Rhodesian Leave*.

The Bodley Head for 'Smoke of the Camp Fire' from *Poems* by BRIAN BROOKE.

Miss E. Bright-Ashford of the Chalice Well Trust and Messrs. Methuen & Co. for 'At the Garden Rail' and 'At Welbedacht' from *The Burden of Engela*, by A. M. BUCKTON.

A. A. Balkema for 'Cape Coloured Batman' and 'Stranger to Europe' from *Stranger to Europe*, and *Africa South* for 'Home Thoughts' by GUY BUTLER.

The Bodley Head for 'The Sling' from *Collected Poems, Vol. 1*; Messrs. Faber and Faber for 'Luis de Camoes' and 'Dreaming Spires' from *Talking Bronco*; Jonathan Cape Ltd. for extracts from *The Flaming Terrapin* and *The Wayzgoose*; Messrs. Curtis Brown Ltd. and Messrs. Faber and Faber for 'The Serf', 'The Zulu Girl', 'The Zebras', 'Rounding the Cape', *from* 'A Veld Eclogue', 'On Some South African Novelists' and 'On the Same', from *Adamastor*, by ROY CAMPBELL.

SYDNEY CLOUTS for 'The Hawk', 'The Sleeper', 'Roy Kloof', 'Roy Kloof went Riding', 'Within', 'The Sea and the Eagle', 'Of Thomas Traherne and the Pebble Outside' and 'The Situation'.

Oxford University Press for 'Resurgat', 'A Pagan's Baptism', 'Lazarus' and 'The Black Christ' from *Africa: Verses* by A. S. CRIPPS.

R. N. Currey for 'Morocco' and 'Marshal Lyautey' and Routledge & Kegan Paul Ltd. for 'Man's Roots', *from* 'Ultimate Exile' and 'Song' from *This Other Planet* and for 'Landscape' from *Indian Landscape*.

Anthony Delius for 'The Explorer', 'The Pilgrims', 'The Gamblers', 'Chameleon'; A. A. Balkema for 'The Coming' from *An Unknown Border*, and *Africa South* for extracts from 'The Great Divide'.

Charles Eglington for 'Cheetah', 'The Vanquished', 'Meeting', and 'Arrival and Departure'.

Oxford University Press for 'The Song Maker' from *Veld Verse* by Kingsley Fairbridge.

Roy Fuller and The Hogarth Press for 'The Green Hills of Africa', 'The Plains', 'The Tribes' and 'In Africa' from *A Lost Season*.

Mrs. N. Podger for 'Jim' by Perceval Gibbon.

Messrs. Philpott and Collins Ltd., Bulawayo, for 'The Councillor' from *From the Outposts*, by Cullen Gouldsbury.

Terence Heywood for 'Cactus', 'Mantis', 'A Flamingo's Egg', 'By an Ant-Heap' and 'Grisaille'.

Peter Jackson for 'In Loco', 'Afrikaans Homestead', 'At the Grave of Cecil Rhodes', 'Great Zimbabwe' and 'Dombashawa'.

Mrs. George Bambridge, Messrs. Methuen & Co. Ltd. and the Macmillan Co. of Canada Ltd. for 'Bridge-Guard in the Karroo' and 'The Burial' from *The Five Nations* by Rudyard Kipling.

L. D. Lerner for 'Senchi Ferry: Gold Coast', 'The Desert Travellers' and '14 July 1956'.

Roy Macnab for 'Child of the Long Grass', 'Majuba Hill', 'The Settler' and *from* 'The Man of Grass'.

Charles Madge for *from* 'Poem by Stages' and Messrs. Faber and Faber Ltd. for 'The Hours of the Planets' and 'Delusions VIII' from *The Disappearing Castle*.

Ruth Miller for 'Fruit', 'Honey', 'Fundisi' and 'The Floating Island'.

Adèle Naudé and A. A. Balkema for 'The Oracle of Delphi' and 'Memling's Virgin with Apple' from *No Longer at Ease*.

Alan Paton for 'Sanna', 'The Discardment', 'Samuel' and 'To a Small Boy who Died at Diepkloof Reformatory'.

JOHN PETER for 'Reading Tolstoy', 'Cypress', 'Christmas on Three Continents', 'Estrangement' and 'Heart's Desire'.

WILLIAM PLOMER and The Hogarth Press Ltd., for 'Johannesburg I', 'The Boer War', 'The Ruined Farm', 'Namaqualand after Rain', 'The Scorpion' from *The Fivefold Screen*; 'The Victoria Falls', 'The Death of a Zulu', 'The Explorer', 'The Pioneers' from *Notes for Poems*; 'A Traveller's Tale' from *Selected Poems*; Jonathan Cape Ltd. for 'The Devil-Dancers' from *Visiting the Caves*; *The New Statesman* for 'A Transvaal Morning'.

F. T. PRINCE and Messrs. Faber and Faber Ltd. for 'In a Province', 'False Bay' and 'Chaka' from *Poems*; The Fortune Press for 'The Babiaantje' from *Soldiers Bathing*.

F. C. SLATER and Messrs. William Blackwood and Sons Ltd. for 'Lament for a Dead Cow', 'The Wood-Gatherers' and 'Milking Kraal' from *Collected Poems*.

ANNE WELSH and The Hand and Flower Press for 'Sight', 'Victoria Dancing' and 'The Body's Eye' from *Uneven World*.

DAVID WRIGHT and André Deutsch Ltd. for 'Seven South African Poems' from *Moral Stories* and 'A Voyage to Africa' from *Monologue of a Deaf Man*.

Thanks are also due to the editors of the following periodicals:

The New Statesman for 'A Transvaal Morning' by WILLIAM PLOMER, '14 July 1956' by L. D. LERNER, and 'The Floating Island' by RUTH MILLER.

The Listener for 'In Memoriam: Roy Campbell' by R. N. CURREY.

English for 'Cactus' by TERENCE HEYWOOD.

London Magazine for 'In Loco', 'Great Zimbabwe', 'Afrikaans Homestead', 'At the Grave of Cecil Rhodes' and 'Dombashawa' by PETER JACKSON.

Encounter for 'Mantis' by TERENCE HEYWOOD.

Poetry, Chicago, for 'A Flamingo's Egg' and 'Grisaille' by TERENCE HEYWOOD.

Trails, U.S.A., for 'By an Ant-Heap' by TERENCE HEYWOOD.

Africa South for extracts from 'The Great Divide' by ANTHONY DELIUS and 'Home Thoughts' by GUY BUTLER.

Standpunte for 'Sight' by ANNE WELSH, 'Majuba Hill' and *from* 'The Man of Grass' by ROY MACNAB, and 'The Sleeper' and 'Within' by SYDNEY CLOUTS.

S.A. Pen Year Book for 'David' by GUY BUTLER and 'The Settler' by ROY MACNAB.

Poetry Commonwealth for 'Durban Revisited' by R. N. CURREY.

West Africa for 'Senchi Ferry: Gold Coast' by L. D. LERNER.

The New Yorker for 'The Gamblers' by ANTHONY DELIUS.

I wish to thank the Librarians of the Cory Library, Rhodes University, Grahamstown; The Africana Library, Johannesburg; The South African Library, Cape Town; and Dr. Killie Campbell of Durban.

INTRODUCTION

I

THERE are slightly over one million English-speaking people in South Africa, scattered over some five hundred thousand square miles. They share this area with a million and a half Afrikaans-speaking compatriots, a million Coloureds and Asiatics, and perhaps ten million Africans. Their poetry, then, is likely to be different from that of other dominions where English has become the only or the dominant language. It is the poetry of a linguistic, political, and cultural minority. In some of her moods the African muse is more fluent in Afrikaans than in English; in certain others she may prefer any one of a dozen African tongues, or the hot, new argot of the townships. Differences of belief and aspiration, as well as speech, have encouraged an intellectual apartheid between these groups. Each has developed along its own lines, suspicious and often tragically ignorant of the others. It should, therefore, be remembered that this volume is devoted to only one of three strands.

The Settlers of 1820 were placed on the frontier between the Dutch pastoralists and the African tribesmen, and, metaphorically speaking, that is where we still are: in the middle. Our small numbers and exposed position have prevented us from developing as strong a national sense as our cousins in other dominions. We speak a form of English which, I believe, shows fewer differences from standard English. Perhaps the sometimes strident anti-British cries of our Afrikaans fellow-countrymen have inclined us to defend inherited ways rather than to develop independent attitudes towards the land of our forefathers. Whatever the causes, the fact remains that, as a group, we lack cultural awareness and make a very half-hearted and ineffective contribution to political life.

> These million English are a vague communion
> Indifferent to leadership or goal,
> Their most accomplished children leave the Union,
> Search other countries for their cause or soul,
> And to the pioneer premise of their fathers
> Add on no better moral, finer story,
> Leave our crude glaring sun and savage weathers
> To bask, reflect in other people's glory.

Thus Anthony Delius. But what market, what audience, can a scattered million be expected to provide for their writers? Our cultural capital is still London, with New York as alternative (we are used to several capitals; the Union has three). We cannot support a single literary periodical. We cannot provide enough teachers to teach our own language to our children. But we are comfortable enough. Because we are economically safe, we simply cannot imagine that we are in any other sort of danger.

Yet this community is waking up. In the last few decades it has certainly produced a fair number of talented writers. The nature of the society to which they belong forces them to work in isolation. Since the Campbell-Plomer adventure with Voorslag,[1] they have never attempted to form a literary school or movement. Many of them migrate. Yet, whether they stay put or get out, they do not usually write about the same things as Australians and New Zealanders.

---

[1] *Voorslag* (Afrikaans—whiplash): *A Monthly Magazine of South African Life and Art*; A. C. Brady, Durban, 1925. Edited by Roy Campbell, who, with William Plomer, contributed heavily to the first two numbers. Laurens van der Post also wrote for the early numbers. The sponsors, frightened by its outspoken tone, tried to interfere with editorial policy. Campbell resigned. 'We returned to England steerage, having been more or less boycotted out of the country after the publication of our magazine, *Voorslag*, which criticized the colour bar' (Campbell: *Light on a Dark Horse*, p. 253). Plomer and van der Post sailed for Japan.

It is interesting to note, however, that visitors like Roy Fuller or Peter Jackson frequently choose to write on the favourite themes of South Africans. This may indicate, among other things, that any developments or changes which one may detect in South African poetry over the past century and a half may be due less to the emergence of a particular local awareness than to changes in Western culture as a whole. It would, in any case, be difficult to determine what 'African' and what 'European' experiences have gone into any poem. It must be stressed that English South Africans are devoid of literary nationalism, and that almost all of their reading comes from across the water. How much this means to some of us 'in these latitudes, with no word, no confraternity, no song' can be gathered from Margaret Allonby's 'A Book for Christmas'.

South African poetry is not, and never has been, a poetry with popular roots. We have no popular songs. If an English South African overseas wants to express *Heimweh* in song, he has to resort to Afrikaans or Zulu. We have no anonymous ballad literature either, no folk songs, although our noisy history is packed with suitable incident. One possible explanation for this silence (as for so much else) is the presence of cheap indigenous labour: it meant that the lonely, ruminative jobs of herding sheep and cattle were done by others; and that the bucolic muse in English was deprived of the mouthpiece which it found in the United States. A stronger factor may have been lack of sufficient time and isolation. Our frontiers were not remote from ports or educational centres for long enough.

South African poetry is, then, an educated man's affair. I cannot detect a peculiar style, or verse form, or intonation. At most one might remark on the frequency of an attribute which Professor G. H. Durrant finds in the work of David

Wright (*Standpunte* XI, 3): 'a simple openness which could not be learned in England'. Many of the best recent poems have a confessional quality about them.

I have made my selection from the work of a number of individuals most of whom are unknown to each other, and some of whom are almost completely unknown in South Africa itself. I searched, in the first instance, for the best verse written by South Africans, and, second, for any good verse written in English which in some way or other deals with the European-African encounter. It was only after I had made my preliminary choice that it struck me as possible to trace the development of certain common themes.

A glance at the biographical notes will reveal that twelve of the thirty-four poets represented here were not born in South Africa. Of these twelve, eight made, or started to make their contribution before the turning-point: the début of Campbell and Plomer in the twenties (i.e. a century after the arrival of the British Settlers). I have devoted less than a fifth of the space available to these forerunners, partly because I think most of them overrated, and partly because there is already an anthology in existence which devotes itself mainly to them (F. Carey Slater's *New Centenary Book of South African Verse*: Longmans).

I have included Kipling among these forerunners. For reasons which escape me he has seldom found a place in South African anthologies, in spite of the fact that these never fail to start off with Pringle, another bird of passage. Pringle's association with Africa was shorter than Kipling's; although that is not the point either. The real point is that Africa touched Kipling to better poetry than Pringle. Mere birth and residence guarantee nothing in art, although they are obviously very important when other factors, such as awareness and talent, are added. As David Wright says:

> What is a man's birthplace? Where the man came forth.
> Not where his embryo, dangerously leaping
> Arrives naked at an accidental hearth.

Of course, things are complicated by the fact that a poet never stops coming forth, being born, becoming aware.

How 'accidental' this 'hearth' may be is well demonstrated by the admittedly unusual case of A. M. Buckton, an English-woman of pro-Boer sympathies, who wrote several volumes of poetry and plays, but whose best work is *The Burden of Engela, A Ballad Epic of the Boer War*. These ballads are the best poems, apart from Kipling's, that we have in English on that disaster. Yet, as far as I can ascertain, she never visited South Africa. Some of the pieces have a concreteness, a reference to the everyday activities of a Transvaal farm (involving at times the use of unusual colloquial expressions unknown to English), which contrasts markedly with her usual rather vague and highflown style. The incidents she dramatized strike me as authentic. I can only assume that her sympathy and imagination were kindled by detailed and circumstantial descriptions.

Of the twenty-three poets who have emerged since the twenties, only four were not born in South Africa. Ten of them, however, have migrated, some in their teens, some in their twenties (Campbell, Plomer, Currey, Prince, Madge, Heywood, Macnab, Peter, Wright and Lerner). Some no longer regard themselves as South Africans. Others return whenever they can. But all have written verse while in this country or verse which owes something to it; either in imagery, or attitude, or preoccupation: e.g., Currey and Wright are frequently concerned with exile. In the case of these *émigrés* I have chosen poems which show this indebtedness. This means that they may not be represented by their best or most mature work, but without some such limitation the title of this volume would have no meaning at all. I have worked in the same way with immigrants and visitors (N. H. Brettell, Roy Fuller, Peter Jackson). With those who were born and live here permanently I have been less restricted in my choice.

II

We are quite accustomed to the idea that the language of poetry cannot remain static; it needs occasional revolutions to fit it for its task of expressing (and sometimes initiating) certain historical changes in society and sensibility. But social structure and sensibility can be changed by a passage across an ocean as well as by a passage of time. A shift in space to a new environment in another hemisphere will sooner or later call for a modification in diction. At the most obvious level it will call for the incorporation of non-English words for local objects or activities, words which, to begin with, will be little more than labels, bizarre-sounding, with no traditional connotations; and later many English words, while approximately appropriate to African objects, will be found to carry overtones either false or equivocal. Both difficulties can be well illustrated from Thomas Pringle, the 'father' of South African poetry.

Pringle was obviously excited by the landscape, races and beasts of Africa. He set about incorporating them into his poetry, borrowing the local Dutch or Kaffir name and explaining it in a footnote where necessary. In the absence of the verbal skill to re-create them, his painstaking catalogues of animals achieve little beyond a sense of strangeness. (Compare the animals in 'Afar in the Desert' with those in Campbell's

'Dreaming Spires'.) On the rare occasions when we pass from versified nature-study to something more exciting, as in the description or rather evocation of the elephants in 'The Desolate Valley', we notice two things. First, the elephant is not new to European poetry; it has been in circulation since Hannibal; it carries at least its own weight in associations. The word is thus not a mere label as *eland* or *quagga* is. (Few African animals have yet been used to really telling effect in poetry, unless, like the lion or the elephant, they have a poetic history behind them, or, as with the aasvogel or jackal, their near relatives (vulture and fox) have. There are exceptions, of course: notably Campbell's 'The Zebras', and the giraffes in his 'Dreaming Spires', N. H. Brettell's 'Giraffe' and Charles Eglington's 'Cheetah'.) Second, the beast and the setting may be wild and bizarre, but the vocabulary is not; it is thoroughly conventional. The passage achieves what atmosphere it has by making the most of the moonlight, pulling out good old romantic stops in phrases like 'wildly beautiful' and 'shadowy solitudes', and metaphors relying on veterans like 'trumpet' and 'kings'.

This conventional diction, and the sensibility that goes with it and which it helps to perpetuate, afflicted South African writing for a century. As already hinted, Pringle himself sometimes got close to realizing the importance of acclimatizing his idiom. In poem after poem his native honesty and sense of fact keep destroying the romantic mood, but without being able to establish an alternative. In his 'Evening Rambles'—a 'twilight' poem in the convention of 'Il Penseroso', 'Grongar Hill' and the 'Ode to Evening'— he gives a perfect demonstration of the perils that beset a poet who attempts to make a conventional European response to what appears to be the appropriate African occasion:

Now along the meadows damp
The enamoured firefly lights his lamp,
Link-boy he of woodland green
To light fair Avon's Elfin queen;
Here, I ween, more wont to shine
To light the thievish porcupine
Plundering my melon-bed—

The anti-climax is comic and charming: the romantic poet
following a cloud of associations generated by 'twilight' realizes
suddenly that in Africa there are not fairies at the bottom of
the garden, but porcupines. Had Pringle's gifts been greater
and his stay in Africa longer, he might have found a barer,
more Wordsworthian vocabulary, have shed some of his stock
responses, and set South African poetry on a path it was to
discover only a century later. As it is, the two generations
of poets who followed him abandoned his laudable struggles
with African objects and animals, and took to high-sounding
waffle, in which Africa or 'the veld' is a vast place so bare
that it offers nothing to distract the poet from the task of
praising or pitying his own soul.

An interesting exception is Charles Barter, who towards the
end of his life wrote his *Stray Memories of Natal and Zululand*
in verse reminiscent of Scott's 'Marmion'. He has a good eye
for detail, and his material is intrinsically interesting. These
two factors, rather than any verbal skill, make him worth
reading. His versification is adequate; it seldom draws attention to itself for downright badness or particular felicity.

In both Barter and Pringle one is very much aware of the
frontier. It lasted longer in Natal than in the Cape, and
longer in Rhodesia than in Natal. Between the eighties and
the Great War this frontier, with its hunters, pioneers, pro-
spectors, railway builders, younger sons and remittance men,
caught the popular imagination, and was celebrated by a
whole school of ballad writers (to whom I should have liked

to give more space) whose model was, of course, Kipling. It is public, usually narrative verse, written to be declaimed and to make an obvious effect. It aims at no verbal subtleties. It has its own clichés, it is often sentimental, but is preferable to the lyrical verse of the time. Several of its practitioners were journalists, with good eyes for an incident or a telling detail. The occasional result is a language close to its subject, a vocabulary which is not embarrassed by railways, rifles, tin cans, and other outriders of Africa's coming industrial revolution. In someone like Gouldsbury it can hint at that disenchantment with both Nature and Progress, and that concern for what is, which is to mark much of the poetry to come.

III

The most obvious change is in the poetic use of the landscape itself. Pringle set the approach for a century. It is an extension of the common Romantic premise that 'God made the country, Man made the town'. The Desert or the Veld is not only uncontaminated by Man; it provides a sense of freedom, of 'something ever more about to be', of a perpetually receding horizon, which the expansive Romantic loves:

> When my bosom is full, and my thoughts are high,
> And my soul is sick with the bondsman's sigh—
> Oh! then there is freedom, and joy, and pride,
> Afar in the desert alone to ride.
> There is rapture to vault on the champing steed
> And to bound away with the eagle's speed
> With the death-fraught firelock in my hand—
> The only law of the desert land.

The last four lines are particularly revealing, for, although the poem ends with a pious 'Man is distant, but God is near', Pringle has acknowledged that the mounted hunter with 'the death-fraught firelock' is lord of those domains: his is 'the only law of the desert land'; and, although he was to campaign ceaselessly against this very fact, he here submits to its appeal, to the rapture of speed, space and violence. Once more, though, his followers chose to develop the conventional strand, until we have Perceval Gibbon at the end of the century ascribing the following sentiments to a transport rider:

> There's a balm for crippled spirits
> In the open view,
> Running from your very footsteps
> Out into the blue;
> Like a wagon track to heaven
> Straight 'twixt God and you. . . .
>
> There's the sum of all religion
> In its mightiness;
> Winged truths, beyond your doubting,
> Close about you press.
> God is greater in the open,—
> Little man is less.

It took a century before the rapture of the hunter, hinted at in Pringle, found its poetic apotheosis in Roy Campbell, so much of whose imagery and ethics derive from that archaic life, with its individualism, self-reliance, stress on courage, physical skill, and endurance of hardship, its acceptance of the cannibal nature of existence, an intimate knowledge of wild beasts, a love of horses and lethal weapons. It should be noted that this way of life was still a reality in the Rhodesia of Campbell's boyhood.

Campbell's values may be derived from the frontier,[1] but there is nothing back-veld or folksy about his verse. His diction and technique are thoroughly sophisticated. His verse is packed with classical and other allusions. For all his rejection

---

[1] 'Hunting and herdsmanship are schools of courage and cunning; they teach self-reliance, individualism, independence. . . . The herdsmen had leisure to dream, and to them civilization owes its poetry, philosophy, astronomy, music, and mathematics.' Campbell, *Portugal*, p. 21.

of the 'bookish muses' of the northern hemisphere, he is obviously soaked in the European tradition. A glance at his invocation to the African muse, from *The Flaming Terrapin*, will show how much of his power springs from his knowledge of both worlds. In many of his most effective images we find some raw, unsophisticated African object yoked to some heavily loaded European image or word: the river Zambesi is given a god in classical fashion, who 'shakes his hoary locks'; the poet's conventional prop, his 'lyre' is strung with 'savage thunder'; the grey baboons are 'gaunt muezzins of the mountain tops'. Like Pringle and Slater, he uses local names, but sparingly and with discretion. But more important than specific techniques is his triumphant introduction of African light and colour and heat into his verse. Other people had talked about these things. Campbell makes us feel them. (Parallels between painters and poets are dangerous, but he reminds me of van Gogh.) He can also create a sense of space and height, of sheer dimension in his poetry, partly by image, partly by resonance and echo. (See extracts II and III from *The Flaming Terrapin*, pp. 34-5.) A lyre of thunder, after all, can only be struck effectively out of doors. It is not likely to be a good instrument for celebrating the delicacies of life.

Few men who have actually hunted or lived as pioneers would subscribe to Gibbon's gentlemanly mystique of the wide open spaces. Campbell, particularly in 'A Veld Eclogue: The Pioneers', ridiculed the nebulous writing it gave rise to. Plomer helped to put paid to this old maid's view of Africa, which made the Karroo and the Bushveld extensions of the Lake District. The landscape is now seen as the face of a Nature which is magnificent, capricious, impersonal. Plomer offers for our contemplation, not 'a primrose by a river's brim' but 'a scorpion on a stone' ('The Scorpion'). Nature is no longer something with which one communes; one watches it with fear and admiration as one might a lion in the open. The Noah extract from *The Flaming Terrapin* evokes the wide open spaces most effectively, but only to assert that Man is the lord of creation, with a mission to bring all things into subjection under his feet:

> There as amid the growing shades he stood
> Facing alone the sky's vast solitude,
> That space, which gods and demons fear to scan,
> Smiled on the proud irreverence of Man.

There is a mystique here too, of course: Man is greater in the open, little God is less. The whole poem can be seen as a celebration of Campbell's belief in primitive courage and vigour, a belief hardly modified by his subsequent conversion to Catholicism.

No South African poet has chosen to develop this particular myth any further, this celebration of 'the pioneer premise of our fathers'. It is a myth difficult to hold once the expanding frontier has disappeared and the glorious spaces are caught under nets of roads, rails, telegraph poles, survey beacons, and stock fences. The innumerable herds of game have been replaced by sheep and cattle whose numbers the farmer has to enter each year on his income tax form. Industry and commerce have brought towns and cities, and these, alas, are populated not by the protagonists of a vital culture, sure of its values, but by those of a decaying one, internally divided, offering to the tribesman, as he steps out of the sorcerer's ring of bones, a choice of beliefs ranging from Catholicism to Communism. A backward glance at Pringle's 'Introductory Stanzas' reveals a moral confidence, a crusading spirit. There is no loss of confidence in Kipling either ('The Burial'). But in some of the verse of the last twenty years we find that the wide open spaces have become the Waste Land, and Europe is seen as the bringer of disease, not of light:

What Gods did you expect to find here, with
What healing powers? What subtle ways of life?
No, there is nothing but the forms and colours,
And the emotion brought from a world already
Dying of what starts to infect the hills.
                (Roy Fuller: 'The Green Hills of Africa')

Africa can offer no help or encouragement: 'there is nothing
but the forms and colours'. It has no history, no gods, no
sages, no art capable of winning our consent or allegiance.
It rejects us.

Once more, Campbell was the first to catch this feeling. In
'Rounding the Cape' he revived the Portuguese myth of
Adamastor, a figure absent from English South African poetry
until he saw its usefulness. Adamastor is the spirit of a barbarous continent resentful of any attempt to disturb its ancient
ignorance and gloom. (It had, in fact, just rejected both
Campbell and Plomer in their spirited attempt in the pages
of *Voorslag* to introduce a little more sweetness and light into
their homeland.) The last two stanzas of the poem reveal Campbell's ambivalent attitude towards Africa which is both 'hated
and adored', and his forebodings in the ominous unease of:

And Night, the Negro, murmurs in his sleep.

But Plomer rather than Campbell is the poet of African
disenchantment. Satirical poems like 'The Boer War', 'The
Pioneers', 'The Explorer', 'Johannesburg', 'The Victoria
Falls', are all intended to prick some bogus provincial senti-
ment about the past or Nature. 'The Scorpion' is particularly
sharp. In his straight pieces Plomer is more sparing and perhaps more precise than Campbell in his use of imagery; his
rhythms are certainly more varied and less insistent. A poem
like 'Namaqualand after Rain' or 'Death of a Zulu' fills one
with regret that he left for Japan as soon as he did.

Plomer was far more prepared than Campbell to experiment

with the new techniques which caught on after World War One. Most of the poets who follow in the thirties are closer technically to Plomer. There is a certain generic similarity between Prince, Currey, Heywood and Madge: restrained, scrupulous in the use of words, intelligent, humane. They all left, and live in England.

IV

The African-European encounter has many facets. In historical terms it meant a series of more or less violent clashes between black and white, and a bitter war between Britain and the Boer Republics; also the rapid industrialization of primitive peoples which followed on the discovery of diamonds and gold. The clashes themselves have produced little good poetry; but the continuous tensions, persisting, have generated some of our best.

The quarrel between the two white races crops up in a hundred Afrikaans poems for every one in English. Most of the readable English poems on the subject are pro-Boer (A. M. Buckton), anti-Imperialistic (Plomer: 'The Boer War'), or attempt an impartial 'reticent sympathy' (Branford: 'Trooper Temple Pulvermacher'; Macnab: 'Majuba'). The satires of Campbell, Plomer and Delius are directed at white South Africa as a whole; they are not racialistic:

> Think not that I on racial questions touch
> For one was British and the other Dutch,

says Campbell. It is, however, a different matter when we deal with Africans and Coloureds.

Pringle came to South Africa with the intention, explicitly avowed in his 'Introductory Stanzas':

> To point the indignant line with heavenly light . . .
> That it Oppression's cruel pride may blight
> By flashing Truth's full blaze on deeds long hid in night.

He has had worthy successors in this: Cripps, Paton, Allonby, Delius, all know how to point an indignant line.

Fighting for 'Afric's race reviled' has proved a difficult task. This is not entirely the fault of white self-interest and un-Christian prejudice: it is quite as much owing to the intimidating distances between primitive tribal life and even the most unsophisticated European existence. Pringle would never admit how great this gap was. Barter emphasized it. The two immigrants to Rhodesia, Gouldsbury and Cripps, stand at opposite poles on this issue. For Cripps the African is the Arcadian, and he describes his 'unspoilt' life in a style which I find inappropriate and sometimes slightly ridiculous. He is at his best when indignant. His indignation, like Paton's, carries a load of irony springing from familiarity with the situation and the habit of testing all situations against the New Testament. Gouldsbury does not idealize the African; he weighs him somewhat laconically, and finds him wanting; a process he extends to whites with similar results. More interesting than either is F. C. Slater, the first South African to write poetry, not verse. Unlike the others, he grew up among Africans; he writes of them as he knew them, without comment. Whereas Pringle is a conscientious and humanitarian Scot describing and reforming a strange land and people, Slater is a Settler descendant singing about them with familiarity and conviction. *The Dark Folk* series, from which I have chosen three pieces, shows a real inventiveness, a sensual awareness of his subjects that leads to the coining of fresh images.

Campbell introduces a new dimension. 'The Serf' and 'The Zulu Girl' have the same actuality as Slater's pieces, but they are more than charming pictures; they are heavy with symbol, resonant, and, like 'Rounding the Cape', they end on an ominous note. This ominous note will be found in a large number of poems in this volume, and, all things considered, it would be surprising if it were not so (see Peter: 'Reading Tolstoy'; Miller: 'The Floating Island'; Clouts: 'The Situation').

It is fairly easy for a European poet to write sympathetically about a Zulu mother, or a coloured child dancing beside a bus queue, but he becomes less sure of himself when faced with groups, with primitive rituals or barbaric customs. This is a side of African life which he must frequently reject or try to ignore. (How much of the charm of F. T. Prince's 'Chaka' would survive if he had chosen to describe his acts from the point of view of a European, and not in a dramatic monologue?) Plomer's 'The Devil-Dancers' catches this sense of civilized bewilderment in the presence of barbarism. Peter Jackson remembers that he is on a continent 'where love in symbols of flowers never prospered, where truth was sorcery'. Roy Fuller's 'The Tribes' makes the same point. Tribal life is cruel, superstitious, irrational; but is the alternative which civilization offers—the jungle of a shanty town—any better?

> The most horrible things you can image are
> Happening in the towns and the most senseless:
> There are no kings or poison,
> Are laws, but no more reason.

V

This clash of cultures forces us to ask questions about culture itself, and makes us rootless.

A South African aware of his European origins, and impatient with much that seems anachronistic in his environment, may disavow the country of his birth and return to the country of his traditions. Once there, however, he may find himself to be an anachronism, and that the England he has sought exists only, say, in Hardy's novels. This may force him to a second disavowal. He ends up outside the consolation of any tradition, with an increased self-knowledge, but stultified by doubts.

> Anachronism and disavowal
> Blurred in the mind . . .
> Shutting us out in the vacancy of truth
> And the present tense
> Where bare feet groped in a donga-bed of drought
> Marred with the forking thorns of our self-pities
> The litter and trash of doubt.
>
> (Peter: 'Estrangement')

It is perhaps no accident that South African poets so frequently assume the masks of Arabs, another imperial people who have attempted to make sense of Africa; or that, like R. N. Currey, they should be fascinated by the French Empire in North Africa, which, as he saw, was to have an increasing relevance to the rest of the continent.

The most recent demonstration of this concern with civilization is Anthony Delius's satire 'The Great Divide'. Technically less infallible than Campbell's South African Satires, it shows a greater anxiety about the things he is determined to defend. Campbell's satire is a trifle too easy, his contempt too absolute. Delius devotes his entire first canto to an analysis of the world scene before turning his attention to his own country. Our disease is general, he finds. We are suffering from a particularly extreme form of it.

Social pressures in South Africa are such that we are forced to examine big words like Liberty, Love, Justice, Truth and Civilization (particularly when coupled with the epithet White). What was a platitude a generation ago, and may still be in England, suddenly becomes startling and immediate here, where it can no longer be taken for granted.

This particular awareness of society has had its effect on

the actual imagery of poetry. In our attempts to depict or assess our situation we have discovered that an historical figure can be turned into a very useful symbol. Campbell was, I think, the first to do this. He uses the name of a Zulu despot not only to symbolize a primitive threat but also heroic and splendid power:

> Armed and crested with a sable plume
> Like a dark cloud clashing a ghostly spear
> The shade of Tchaka strides across the gloom.

So, too, Rhodes and Kruger are used to represent groups and their attitudes. Certain great missionaries—symbolizing as they can be made to do, many Western values—are becoming increasingly popular in poetry (Delius: 'The Explorer'; Macnab: 'The Man of Grass').

The most important and most frequently-used symbol to emerge in recent South African verse (apart from the sun) is that of the traveller through strange lands and among strange peoples; an exile, who by deprivation of the familiar and immersion in a bewildering plurality, is forced to explore his own and others' assumptions and values. It is a natural enough symbol in a multi-racial country where a European must often feel exiled, and where exploration ceased fairly recently. (It is also one of the oldest devices in the world: poetry abounds in quests and voyages.) Noah in *The Flaming Terrapin* is taken on one such voyage. It is, however, less a voyage of discovery than an endurance test. Plomer's 'A Traveller's Tale' is the first of a long succession of imaginary or real journeys into the mystery. Charles Madge's 'Poem by Stages' is packed with cultural comparisons and uncertainties. Delius's 'The Travellers', David Wright's 'A Voyage to Africa', L. D. Lerner's 'The Desert Travellers', are all poems of reassessment of self and of the world. Here is Wright addressing the island of St. Helena:

We, the visitants, the immigrants, and those
Who, fed with the familiar, demand the same
In new environs, but at a lower price,
Thus wandering down a groove, always become
At a point of a voyage, or of our lives,

Aware we are looking back no longer to
Where we have come from, but must begin to plan
Arrival at those places to which we go—
As you, stark island, who marry European
To African dilapidation, seem to do.

('A Voyage to Africa')

A related device is to contemplate Africa from Europe (Butler: 'Home Thoughts') or, in some taciturn African setting, to consider what Europe means—a favourite method of Peter Jackson. Currey in 'Man's Roots' comes to the conclusion that

Man's roots are not in earth . . .
But, as a ship, or migrant bird, or deer
Moves in a limited orbit, driving back
On predetermined courses, so with man;
His many-branching lungs are roots in air;
His eyes, mind, lips have roots; and he is drawn
By vital tissues, dying if they crack.

I think this is pretty typical. South African English poets never talk about being rooted in African soil. Campbell's 'The Land Grabber' perhaps overstates their caution:

On a Poet who offered His Heart for
a Handful of South African Soil

The bargain is fair and the bard is no robber,
A handful of dirt for a heart full of slobber.

Sydney Clouts has dramatized the tension we feel between Europe and Africa in the figure of Roy Kloof. Roy Kloof's mother is English and is seen in the landscape of an English shire, with cottage gardens and castles on hills. His father is Afrikaans, and farms a stony soil. Their divorce solves nothing for their son, who can side with neither without impoverishment and pain:

> . . . I cried and I cried
> Till rock and shire were divorced.
> Division incarnate! An unhappy rôle:
> My country has given me a flint for a soul.
> (Clouts: 'Roy Kloof')

There are times when the 'shire' and the world it represents (the legendary richness of Europe, its historical alluvium) seem false and inappropriate, and the semantic poverty and nakedness of Africa's 'rock' seems preferable: as to H. C. Bosman:

> . . . Instead of a sky panoplied
> With flighted images I'd sooner have
> A mealie-field to gaze upon; I would try
> To keep the growing earth within the sound
> Of my blood. The Fates were careless when they gave
> Me these banished things in superfluity—
> Lost facts brooding like temples instead of ground
> For seed and harvest.
> ('The Poet')

Most of our poets have tried to belong to Africa, and, finding her savage, shallow and unco-operative, have been forced to give their allegiance, not to any other country, but to certain basic conceptions. In their searchings and journeys they have, naturally enough, 'driven back on predetermined courses' to their European origins. What rest or stability they find is not in any particular place, but on principles: the integrity of the individual; the duty to seek the truth and proclaim it; the command to love thy neighbour. All these concepts are alien to an Africa

> Indifferent to love or hate
> Incomprehensible to placate
> (Peter: 'Christmas on Three Continents')

These 'European' principles are difficult to transplant among tribesmen, particularly when Europeans themselves tend to lose them. We have to re-discover and realize them afresh in their African context. Like Delius's Livingstone, we frequently find ourselves

> bent above the growing chart
> Of savage and amazing truth.

The experience is succinctly put by Peter Jackson:

> The way of time
> Is exigency eating at the legend
> Of our love and truth: not the old mysteries
> Make fear, but to the still discovering mind
> The simple penance of such words brought home.

It is not therefore surprising that much recent South African poetry is inward, Our journeys bring us back to ourselves. As with Delius's pilgrim,

> through a second's split he stares
> at what he went so far to find,
> the sanctuary's inner veil
> hangs at the back of every mind.

Not all the poetry emerging from this sanctuary has a confessional or credal quality; one does occasionally hear a *gloria*, a joyous assent of the whole being, springing from some deeply felt relationship. The world of measurement and analysis pales before immediate experience:

> I had dispensed with numbers; finding how
> Since Space was always Here and Time was Now,
> Extent of either means a Fig to me;
> To the whole field I can prefer a flower
> And know that States are foundered by an hour
> While centuries may groan to fell a tree.

> By its cool guidance I unread my books
> And learned, in spite of theories and charts,
> Things have a nearer meaning to their looks
> Than to their dead analyses in parts;
> And how (for all the outfit be antique)
> Our light is in our heads, and we can seek
> The clearest information in our hearts.
>
> (Campbell: 'The Sling')

This is, of course, little more than Blake's insistence on the wisdom of particularity; and certainly without it poetry cannot exist. In its intenser manifestations, it involves a radical destruction, which precedes fresh vision. At such times,

> seasons overrule the calendars,—
> Image is put to question by the eye.
> (Welsh: 'The Body's Eye')

Much poetry is born in this disputed territory between the current formula and the fresh sensation, where new experiences flood and baptize the intellectual frontiers, and where intellect reasserts a new and modified control. Sometimes one can express little more than an awareness of the new experience and the difficulty of reducing it to words:

> What pendulum can trace the mind's unseen
> Sharp arcs, its blind man's reach
> Round knots of being that have never been
> Subdued to slip through flaming hoops of speech?
> (Butler: 'Home Thoughts')

At others it leads to an understanding, a symbiosis, as in Margaret Allonby's 'Reflection'.

VI

Thus, if a search for meaning leads to a certain detachment from society and country, it also leads, paradoxically, to a sharper or different sensual awareness of the world. This, as always, results in a 'return to Nature'. The motives for this return are various and complex, but a hunger for innocence, for the completeness of an amoral, instinctive existence, is powerful among them. Nature is no longer like Plomer's in 'The Scorpion'. It has more affinities with Campbell's

> great machine
> Thoughtless and fearless, governing the clean
> System of active things.
> (*The Flaming Terrapin*)

xxxviii

Nature is pre-lapsarian, clean. Animals know neither good nor evil, are as innocent as

> Engines of beauty volted with delight
> ('The Zebras')

and for this reason they are to be looked at with envy and reverence. This is fairly recent, and may owe something to the fact that the beasts are now completely at our mercy, not we at theirs. They exist by our grace in game reserves. There must be a difference in attitude between an ivory hunter, with rifle, and a visitor to a park, with camera. Compare Brooke's 'Smoke of the Camp Fire' with Brettell's 'Elephant'. As Fuller reminds us, 'the lives of lions now are made shabby with rifles'.

Having conquered Nature we have abolished a favourite hiding place of our own fears and wishes. We are without disguise or clothing. But nakedness is no longer natural to us, and we have to assume masks and disguises to be ourselves, to know ourselves. This can no longer be an unconscious or half-conscious process. We know what we are about. So, writing of Nature, Wright says:

> A mirror more perfect than any of glass
> She is; when looked in, the looker sees a shape
> Of his emotion, and of what really was
> There looking in: of an angel or an ape. . . .
>
> O Nature, mirror or mishandled pantry
> Or medicine, goddess, enemy, what you like,
> I love you, and knowing whom I really love
> I find it difficult not to love you more:
> Either in a city's confines, at one remove,
> Or when I travelling past in a train or car
> Touch the innocence your wildernesses prove.
> ('A Voyage to Africa')

'Innocent' is a frequent epithet. It is applied to the cactus by both Heywood ('Cactus') and Jackson ('In Loco'). Brettell's giraffes are 'innocent, epicene'.

But a glance at Heywood's 'By an Ant-Heap', Clout's 'The Hawk' or Eglington's 'Cheetah', will show that, if it is innocence, it is innocence with a difference. Clouts, in 'The Sea and the Eagle', makes Wright's point again: the inescapable anthropomorphism of our approaches to the world.

> We have given you both a mystery.
> Reveal it and we shall see ourselves
> Suddenly like a rising wing,
> Terribly like a swoop of water.

A landscape where 'there is nothing but the forms and the colours' (Fuller) desperately needs man to give it a mystery, to read something into it. It is a prerequisite of poetry, if not of life. It will also lead inevitably to more 'myths' and to 'that damned fatality, an eyelit world' (Jackson).

Our awareness of what we are up to, that we are reading things into the world, makes us self-conscious and cautious in our imagery, but it has interesting and exciting possibilities, e.g. the conscious selection and development of a symbol to suggest or explore a feeling. Thus Madge:

> Among all the myths and masks and make-believes
> Is the solid marvel of the antique bed,
> A decent idol. Long washed in the tides
> Of the spring estuary, the salted stone
> Is big and smooth. Abundant are the waters.
> I can rest here, the waves lapping beside.
> And all dead things all corpses and corruptions
> Are cleansed into a flotsam of hard shapes
> Are in reversion are made whole again. . . .

'A decent idol.' In her remarkable poem, 'Reflection', Margaret Allonby uses images in a more elaborate way as a means of exploration and definition, and with the same caution; she is 'Aware experience is not innocence', and that her insight comes 'in chanciness of myth'.

This caution springs in part from a realization of human finiteness, and of perpetual change. Both demand growth and adaptation. **Because** we are not complete, it is death to stop in any sort of absoluteness.

> Death or dishevelment we are constrained
> By this one universe to look beyond
> Images crusted with time's accretions.
> (Welsh: 'The Body's Eye')

Only in finding the right image, an image which is a clear reflection of ourselves in the world and the world in us, do we achieve, however briefly, a homecoming.

VII

It is not necessarily to a poet's advantage to be introduced to new readers in company with a score or more fellow poets, particularly when the opening remarks have emphasized what they have in common, not what distinguishes them. It is an individual voice, not a family profile or national trait, which makes a poet. But individual attention to authors or poems is obviously out of the question in an introduction of this sort.

I decided, after considerable hesitation, to work on the principle of representing each poet by more than one piece. This meant, in effect, excluding several people I should have liked to include, but I felt that it was better to give a few people as reasonable a hearing as an anthology would allow, than to include so many that none had the chance of making an impression.

I have tried in most cases to give a representative selection from each poet I have chosen, not limiting myself to anthology pieces, but including at least one difficult or longer poem which might better suggest the poet's depth or range.

Grahamstown, 1958.   GUY BUTLER

THOMAS PRINGLE

The Emigrants
Introductory Stanzas

Sweet Teviot, fare thee well! Less gentle themes
Far distant call me from thy pastoral dale,
To climes where Amakosa's woods and streams
Invite, in the fair South, my venturous sail.
There roaming sad the solitary vale,
From native haunts and early friends exiled,
I tune no more the string for Scottish tale;
For to my aching heart, in accents wild,
Appeals the bitter cry of Afric's race reviled.

From Keissi's meads, from Chumi's hoary woods,
Bleak Tarka's dens, and Stormberg's rugged fells,
To where Gareep pours down his sounding floods
Through regions where the hunted Bushman dwells,
That bitter cry wide o'er the desert swells,
And, like a spirit's voice, demands the song
That of these savage haunts the story tells—
A tale of foul oppression, fraud, and wrong,
By Afric's sons endured from Christian Europe long.

Adieu, ye lays to youthful fancy dear!
Let darker scenes a sterner verse inspire,
While I attune to strains that tyrants fear
The deeper murmurs of the British lyre,—

And from a holier altar ask the fire
To point the indignant line with heavenly light,
(Though soon again in darkness to expire,)
That it oppression's cruel pride may blight,
By flashing TRUTH's full blaze on deeds long hid in night!

THOMAS PRINGLE

Afar in the Desert[1]

Afar in the desert I love to ride,
With the silent Bush-boy alone by my side:
When the sorrows of life the soul o'ercast,
And, sick of the Present, I cling to the past;
When the eye is suffused with regretful tears,
From the fond recollections of former years;
And shadows of things that have long since fled
Flit over the brain, like the ghosts of the dead:
Bright visions of glory—that vanished too soon;
Day dreams—that departed ere manhood's noon;
Attachments—by fate or by falsehood reft;
Companions of early days—lost or left;

[1] 'Though at the time so busy that I had not looked at any of the new books, I was so completely taken possession of that for some days I did little else but read and recite your poem, now to this group and now to that, and since that time have either written, or caused to be written, at least half a dozen copies. . . . I do not hesitate to declare it among the two or three most perfect lyric poems in our language.' S. T. Coleridge, letter to Pringle, quoted from the Memoir written by Leitch Ritchie.

'A writer in the Union number of *The Times* (5 Nov. 1910) endeavoured to correct the current over-valuation of his (Pringle's) poetry. After quoting the term "inspired doggerel", applied to *Afar in the Desert* by Oscar Wilde, he referred to the poem as "not a remarkable production".' Miller and Sergeant, *Survey of South African Poetry*, Balkema, 1957.

And my native Land—whose magical name
Thrills to the heart like electric flame;
The home of my childhood; the haunts of my prime;
All the passions and scenes of that rapturous time
When the feelings were young and the world was new,
Like the fresh flowers of Eden unfolding to view;
All—all now forsaken—forgotten—foregone!
And I—a lone exile remembered by none—
My high aims abandoned,—my good acts undone,—
Aweary of all that is under the sun,—
With that sadness of heart which no stranger may scan,
I fly to the desert, afar from man!

Afar in the desert I love to ride,
With the silent Bush-boy alone by my side:
When the wild turmoil of this wearisome life,
With its scenes of oppression, corruption, and strife—
The proud man's frown, and the base man's fear,—
The scorner's laugh, and the sufferer's tear,—
And malice, and meanness, and falsehood, and folly,
Dispose me to musing and dark melancholy;
When my bosom is full, and my thoughts are high,
And my soul is sick with the bondsman's sigh—
Oh! then there is freedom, and joy, and pride,
Afar in the desert alone to ride!
There is rapture to vault on the champing steed,
And to bound away with the eagle's speed,
With the death-fraught firelock in my hand—
The only law in the Desert Land!

Afar in the desert I love to ride,
With the silent Bush-boy alone by my side:
Away, away, from the dwellings of men,

By the wild deer's haunt, by the buffalo's glen;
By valleys remote where the oribi plays,
Where the gnu, the gazelle, and the hartebeest graze,
And the kùdù and eland unhunted recline
By the skirts of grey forests o'erhung with wild vine;
Where the elephant browses at peace in his wood,
And the river-horse gambols unscared in the flood,
And the mighty rhinoceros wallows at will
In the fen where the wild ass is drinking his fill.

Afar in the desert I love to ride,
With the silent Bush-boy alone by my side:
O'er the brown Karroo, where the bleating cry
Of the springbok's fawn sounds plaintively;
And the timorous quagga's shrill whistling neigh
Is heard by the fountain at twilight grey;
Where the zebra wantonly tosses his mane,
With wild hoof scouring the desolate plain;
And the fleet-footed ostrich over the waste
Speeds like a horseman who travels in haste,
Hieing away to the home of her rest
Where she and her mate have scooped their nest,
Far hid from the pitiless plunderer's view
In the pathless depths of the parched Karroo.

Afar in the desert I love to ride,
With the silent Bush-boy alone by my side:
Away, away, in the wilderness vast,
Where the white man's foot hath never passed,
And the quivered Coránna or Bechuán
Hath rarely crossed with his roving clan:
A region of emptiness, howling and drear,
Which man hath abandoned from famine and fear;

Which the snake and the lizard inhabit alone,
With the twilight bat from the yawning stone;
Where grass, nor herb, nor shrub takes root,
Save poisonous thorns that pierce the foot;
And the bitter-melon, for food and drink,
Is the pilgrim's fare by the salt lake's brink:
A region of drought, where no river glides,
Nor rippling brook with osiered sides;
Where sedgy pool, nor bubbling fount,
Nor tree, nor cloud, nor misty mount,
Appears, to refresh the aching eye:
But the barren earth, and the burning sky,
And the blank horizon, round and round,
Spread—void of living sight and sound,
And here, while the night-winds round me sigh,
And the stars burn bright in the midnight sky,
As I sit apart by the desert stone,
Like Elijah at Horeb's cave alone,
'A still small voice' comes through the wild
(Like a father consoling his fretful child),
Which banishes bitterness, wrath, and fear,—
Saying—MAN IS DISTANT, BUT GOD IS NEAR!

THOMAS PRINGLE

From *The Desolate Valley*

. . . Then, couched at night in hunter's wattled shieling,
How wildly beautiful it was to hear
The elephant his shrill *reveillé* pealing

Like some far signal trumpet on the ear!
While the broad midnight moon was shining clear,
How fearful to look forth upon the woods,
And see those stately forest-kings appear,
Emerging from their shadowy solitudes—
As if that trump had woke Earth's old gigantic broods.

Such the majestic, melancholy scene
Which midst that mountain wilderness we found;
With scarce a trace to tell where man had been,
Save the old Kafir cabins crumbling round.
Yet this lone glen (Sicana's ancient ground)[1]
To Nature's savage tribes abandoned long,
Had heard, erewhile, the Gospel's joyful sound
And low of herds mixed with the Sabbath song.
But all is silent now. The Oppressor's hand was strong.[2]

Now the blithe loxia hangs her pensile nest
From the wild olive, bending o'er the rock,
Beneath whose shadow, in grave mantle drest
The Christian pastor taught his swarthy flock.
A roofless ruin, scathed by flame and smoke,
Tells where the decent Mission-chapel stood;
While the baboon with jabbering cry doth mock
The pilgrim, pausing in his pensive mood
To ask: 'Why is it thus? Shall Evil baffle Good?' . . .

[1] A secondary chief or captain of a Kafir hamlet at the Kat River was one of the converts of the missionary Williams. This remarkable man composed the first Christian hymn, or sacred song, ever expressed in his native tongue.

[2] Refers to the devastation of the wars of 1818 and 1819, when the Caffres and Ghonaquas (Hottentots) converted by Williams were 'forced to become bondmen among the Boers, or imprisoned on Robben Island' (Pringle).

Look round that Vale: behold the unburied bones
Of Ghona's children withering in the blast.[1]
The sobbing wind, that through the forest moans
Whispers: 'The spirit hath forever passed!'
Thus in the Vale of Desolation vast
In moral death dark Afric's myriads lie;
But the Appointed Day shall dawn at last
When, breathed on by a Spirit from on High
The dry bones shall awake, and shout: 'Our God is nigh!'

CHARLES BARTER

From *Stray Memories of Natal and Zululand*

Dingaan and Retief[2]

LXXXIV

Two regiments surround the throne;
In solid semi-circle shewn;

[1] See footnote [2] p. 6.

[2] Shaka or Chaka, the Attila of Africa, started life as a despised exile and outcast. He built up the Zulu 'empire' by relentless cruelty and military genius, depopulating vast tracts in the process. Powerful tribes who refused to be 'eaten', moved south, to set up a chain reaction which disturbed the frontiers of the Cape; others, notably those under the leadership of Mosilikatze, went North, to terrorize Central Africa, and to found the Matabele kingdom, which was destroyed by the British in 1893. Their last great king, Lobengula, was another exile-adventurer.

Chaka was murdered in 1828 by his half-brothers Dingaan and Mhlangana. The former soon had the latter assassinated, and made himself king.

Dingaan appears to have been even more bloody-minded than Chaka. In 1837 he murdered Piet Retief, the leader of the first party of trekkers to enter Natal. The next year, at Blood River, the Boers inflicted a crippling defeat on his *impis*. Panda, another of his brothers, encouraged and helped by the Boers, rose in rebellion and overthrew him. Retreating into Swaziland, Dingaan was captured by Sobuza, and tortured to death.

Their names, the black shields, and the white,
The latter vet'rans, skill'd in fight,
The pick of all the Zulu host,
Loud, but not idle, is their boast.
The ring upon the shaven crown
Mark them as men of high renown;
None but tried servants of the King
Have leave to wear the marriage ring
Of bark and grass and wax combined,
And tightly with the wool entwined.
A younger race the black shields bear;
Cropp'd but not shaven, is their hair
The knob kerrie their only arm
Short, heavy, fit for deadly harm.
Dingaan was seated in his pride,
A councillor on either side,
As the old farmer chief drew near,
He greeted him with words of cheer,
Hop'd friendly feelings would endure
Between his people and the Boer,
And that his countrymen would come
And make Natal their settled home:
Wished him a pleasant journey there,
And pledged him in a draught of beer.

LXXXV

Sudden, above the voices loud,
The shouts and clamour of the crowd,
The traitor's cruel voice is heard,
'Seize them!' he cries, and at the word,
Hurl'd to the earth each guest lies prone,
By weight and numbers backward thrown.

. . . They dragged them to a neighb'ring hill,
Whether for euphony or grace
Misnam'd the soldier's muster place:
Gehenna were its fitter name;
A place of death, and dread, and shame!
The work of slaughter then began;
No mortal combat, man to man,
But ten to one; the blows fell fast,
As hail before the whirling blast,
That falls upon a field of corn,
And leaves it barren and forlorn!
The shatter'd skull, the spouting brain,
The red blood oozing o'er the plain,
The hands outstretched towards the sky
Or clench'd in dying agony,
The eyes that with mad phrenzy glare,
The sullen look of dull despair,
All these, and fouler sights, were there!

And he, their leader and their guide,
Of the brave Boers the boast and pride. . . .
His raiment torn, his forehead scarr'd,
His face by pain and horror marr'd
His grey hairs waving in the wind,
Compell'd by cruelty refin'd
To stand and witness, ere he die,
Each detail of the butchery:
As one by one his comrades all
Like oxen 'neath the pole-axe fall. . . .
The bitterness of mortal pain

He tasted o'er and o'er again:
While at his heart-strings fell remorse
Is tugging with resistless force,
And brings the overwhelming thought,
'Twas he this havoc who had wrought,
'Twas he the words of warning spurn'd,
Else had they all in peace returned. . . .
When all was o'er, he met his fate,
As one who grudg'd its coming late,
Whether by torture keen and slow
Or yielding to a mortal blow,
No records say; they only tell
That last of all his band, he fell.

LXXXVIII

Yet was he spar'd a deeper woe,
What was not yet, he could not know,
He did not hear the dying scream
Of women by Umtyezi's stream;
The shriller shrieks he did not hear
Of children, writhing on the spear,
Of infants swinging by the heel,
Then dash'd against the wagon wheel;
Moord Spruit had not been nam'd as yet,
Nor till more late, did Weenen get
From weeping wives and sires its name,
Since enter'd on the roll of fame!
He knew not that five hundred more
Would soon be added to the score
Of Dutch by Zulus trapp'd and slain:
Nor that their blood was shed in vain.

But for the blood so foully shed
Did the vengeance follow, deep and dread,
Nor long delay'd: ere yet the sun
Through the twelve signs his course had run,
Dingaan, a mighty king no more
His reign of blood and carnage o'er,
Three thousand men in battle lost,
And chas'd by Panda's rebel host,
Discrowned, deserted, and betrayed,
Was captive by Sobuza made.
There, in a darksome hut immur'd
Three days of torture he endur'd.
The first, by sharpest points of steel
His skin was pierc'd from head to heel:
The next, by dogs his flesh was torn;
The third, by pain and hunger worn,
And when the spear had pierc'd his eyes,
In darkness and despair he dies.

Changes

XXXI

Thence onward by the well-known road
My horse's feet had often trod
In former years, when, gun in hand,
I first explor'd this border land:
When Walmsley held Tugela's side,
And all the Zulu host defied:
When under Hlatikulu's shade
The buffalos in safety play'd;
When every night, beneath the moon,
The sea cows, in the still lagoon,

Rear'd their huge heads above the stream,
Or plunged below with flashing gleam.
How chang'd the scene! The silent lane
Is clogged with loads of ripen'd cane;
For murmur of the trickling rill,
The clang and shock of throbbing mill:
And where his wives saw Tshaka die
A bustling, thriving hostelry.

XXXV

Well I remember now the scene
Through mists of years that intervene;
The wagons on the sunburnt grass,
The mounted troopers as they pass:
Oxen and mules, a mingled throng,
By naked kafirs urged along;
The drivers, with unearthly shout,
Horses with saddles and without;
Men mounting·in hot haste, to gain
Their places in the length'ning train;
All is in wild confusion tost:
Another gaze—the scene is lost.
And what remains? The trodden ground,
The dusty eddies circling round;
The whitewash'd building on the hill,
The trees that look so lone and still,
The swift Umgeni rushing by,
The calmness of the winter sky.

RUDYARD KIPLING

Bridge-Guard in the Karroo

'and will supply details to guard the Blood River Bridge.'
District Orders: Lines of Communication—South African War.

Sudden the desert changes,
    The raw glare softens and clings,
Till the aching Oudtshoorn ranges
    Stand up like the thrones of kings—

Ramparts of slaughter and peril—
    Blazing, amazing, aglow—
'Twixt the sky-line's belting beryl
    And the wine-dark flats below.

Royal the pageant closes,
    Lit by the last of the sun—
Opal and ash-of-roses,
    Cinnamon, umber, and dun.

The twilight swallows the thicket,
    The starlight reveals the ridge;
The whistle shrills to the picket—
    We are changing guard on the bridge.

(Few, forgotten and lonely,
    Where the empty metals shine—
No, not combatants—only
    Details guarding the line.)

13

We slip through the broken panel,
　Of fence by the ganger's shed;
We drop to the waterless channel
　And the lean track overhead;

We stumble on refuse of rations,
　The beef and the biscuit-tins;
We take our appointed stations,
　And the endless night begins.

We hear the Hottentot herders
　As the sheep click past to the fold—
And the click of the restless girders
　As the steel contracts in the cold—

Voices of jackals calling
　And, loud in the hush between,
A morsel of dry earth falling
　From the flanks of the scarred ravine.

And the solemn firmament marches,
　And the hosts of heaven rise
Framed through the iron arches—
　Banded and barred by the ties,

Till we feel the far track humming,
　And we see her headlight plain,
And we gather and wait her coming—
　The wonderful north-bound train.

(Few, forgotten and lonely,
　Where the white car-windows shine—
No, not combatants—only
　Details guarding the line.)

Quick, ere the gift escape us!
    Out of the darkness we reach
For a handful of week-old papers
    And a mouthful of human speech.

And the monstrous heaven rejoices,
    And the earth allows again,
Meetings, greetings, and voices
    Of women talking with men.

So we return to our places,
    As out on the bridge she rolls;
And the darkness covers our faces,
    And the darkness re-enters our souls.

More than a little lonely
    Where the lessening tail-lights shine.
No—not combatants—only
    Details guarding the line!

RUDYARD KIPLING

The Burial

1902

(*C. J. Rhodes, buried in the Matoppos, 10 April 1902*)

When that great Kings return to clay,
    Or Emperors in their pride,
Grief of a day shall fill a day,
    Because its creature died.

But we—we reckon not with those
  Whom the mere Fates ordain,
This Power that wrought on us and goes
  Back to the Power again.

Dreamer devout, by vision led
  Beyond our guess or reach,
The travail of his spirit bred
  Cities in place of speech.
So huge the all-mastering thought that drove—
  So brief the term allowed—
Nations, not words, he linked to prove
  His faith before the crowd.

It is his will that he look forth
  Across the world he won—
The granite of the ancient North—
  Great spaces washed with sun.
There shall he patient make his seat
  (As when the Death he dared),
And there await a people's feet
  In the paths that he prepared.

There, till the vision he foresaw
  Splendid and whole arise,
And unimagined Empires draw
  To council 'neath his skies,
The immense and brooding Spirit still
  Shall quicken and control.
Living he was the land, and dead,
  His soul shall be her soul!

A. M. BUCKTON

At the Garden Rail

'Tis strange that absence often does
    What presence cannot do!
Since Piet is back,[1] I mark in him
    Old things I never knew.

I went to meet him yester eve;
    The honey sky was pale,
The scented parsley filled the air
    Beyond the garden rail.

The men were braying[2] cattle-hides
    All day within the kraal;
The maidens stripping mealie cobs
    In rows beneath the wall.

Piet was dipping mountain stock
    Upon the higher slope:
'Tis three days since he started forth
    With casting net and rope.

He holds it good: though Ouma[3] says
    'No pagan wash can keep
The scab away, if 'tis His will
    To doom a flock of sheep!'

[1] Boers on commando were given leave to return to their farms to plough or do work which their womenfolk found too difficult.

[2] Braying: from Afrikaans *brei*, to dress or curry skins. Men and maidens, African farm labourers.

[3] Ouma: grandmother.

17

She sighs and chides him like a child,
    Lifting her agèd hand;
But if the world is good enough,
    Why till and plough the land?

I looked abroad upon the fields—
    The father lingers late!
When lo, I saw him in the dusk,
    Staggering to the gate.

A new-born calf upon his back—
    He carried it alone;
The mother followed, licking it,
    With tender anxious moan:
What was there in the sight to make
    My foolish tears to run?

A. M. BUCKTON

At Welbedacht

'The stallions I must have, good wife! the red one and the
    brown.
'Twill be to your advantage, too, to send them saddled down
Into the camp tonight; if not, be sure I come at morn!'

She stood at the open door, alone, in her widow's dress;
She saw them ride away—she knew her loneliness,
And turned and wrung her hands. 'My God—spare me this!'

'The red and the brown, he said? Nay, take the rest o' the
    stall!
Foals my husband bred, and prized the most of all,
To bear strange men, and ride to the enemy's bugle call!'

. . . She sat till the sun went down; and waited for the night:
She looked to the distant camp, where the fires flickered bright;
Then silently she rose, and fetched a stable light.

The children slumbered both: she bent above the bed;
She took the leathern case from under the mattress head,
And slowly turned her steps behind the cattle-shed.

The creatures heard her foot, and whinnied to see her stand:
She loosed the halters, and gave the open fondling hand. . . .
Nay, finer foals were never foaled in any land!

She led to the open manger; she tethered the lantern fast,
And mixed the ready mash. 'Though it should be our last,'
She cried, 'we will have to-night our joy of this repast!'

Their lips and nostrils quivered to feel the wholesome corn;
She combed their massy manes with a comb of yellow horn:
'We must be ready, ready to meet the coming morn.'

She looked abroad from the threshold: the dawn was very near!
The manger-meal was done: why did she linger there?
She turned her into the stable, steady, without a fear. . . .

Four pistol-shots rang out in the silence of the night—
The cow-boy started forth from his hut in sudden fright,
And met a reeling woman bearing a stable-light.

.   .   .   .   .

Two troopers came at dawn, with a sergeant at their head.
'Yield us the stallions, woman! the brown one and the red!'
She gazed as one that wanders: 'Take them,' was all she said.

A. S. CRIPPS

Resurgat

(for C. J. Rhodes)

God be with you in your need!
When God's mills have ground you through—
All the coarse cruel chaff of you—
Be there left one grain to sow,
Which in season may unfold
Your visionary might of old!

Vine-dresser of the world-to-be,
Leave not one branch, yet leave the tree
Its life abounding, leave it free
Like some fecund vine to sprawl
On the widths of Sion's wall
In penitence imperial!

A. S. CRIPPS

A Pagan's Baptism

Dread Potter, in Thine hands we lay
Thine image made—and marred—in clay.
First, in Thy timely mercy break:
Then all re-make!

These votive waters wait Thee here—
'Twixt rocks and greensward—deep and clear:
Water and dust we give for share;
Give fire and air!

That Tree Thou barest lit for earth
Her Furnace flame of cleansing worth:
In crimson hollow of Thine Hand
That flame be fanned!

Breathe, Air, from out the land desired;
Breathe till this glowing clay be fired!
According to Thy primal plan
Create a man!

A. S. CRIPPS

Lazarus

I watched him at the banquet wait—
The drunken banquet grossly plann'd—
The serf who held his master's fate
In hollow of his swarthy hand.

Dim purple hangings he had draped,
Had blanched fine linen smooth and fair,
The meats had dressed, the bake-meats shaped:
A cuff, a curse he took for share.

O dark, meek Mephistopheles,
Safe in your hand a soul you hold:
Th' inevitable end he sees
No more than Dives saw of old.

A. S. CRIPPS

The Black Christ

(At Easter in South Africa)

Pilate and Caiaphas
They have brought this thing to pass—
That a Christ the Father gave,
Should be guest within a grave.

Church and State have willed to last
This tyranny not over-past;
His dark-southern Brows around
They a wreath of briars have bound;
In His dark despised Hands
Writ in sores their writing stands.

By strait starlit ways I creep,
Caring while the careless sleep,
Bearing balms, and flow'rs to crown

That poor Head the stone holds down:
Through some crack or crevice dim
I would reach my sweets to Him.

Easter suns they rise and set,
But that stone is steadfast yet:
Past my lifting 'tis, but I
When 'tis lifted would be nigh.

I believe, whate'er they say,
The sun shall dance one Easter Day,
And I, that through thick twilight grope
With balms of faith and flow'rs of hope,
Shall lift mine eyes, and see the stone
Stir and shake, if not be gone.

F. C. SLATER

Lament for a Dead Cow

(Chant by Xhosa family on the death of Wetu, their only cow)

Siyalila, siyalila, inkomo yetu ifile! [1]
   Beautiful was Wetu as a blue shadow,
That nests on the grey rocks
About a sunbaked hilltop:
Her coat was black and shiny
Like an isipingo-berry;
Her horns were as sharp as the horns of the new moon
That tosses aloft the evening star;

---

[1] We weep, we weep, our cow is dead!

Her round eyes were as clear and soft
As a mountain-pool,
Where shadows dive from the high rocks.
No more will Wetu banish teasing flies
With her whistling tail;
No more will she face yapping curs
With lowered horns and bewildered eyes;
No more will her slow shadow
Comfort the sunburnt veld, and her sweet lowing
Delight the hills in the evening.
The fountain that filled our calabashes
Has been drained by a thirsty sun;
The black cloud that brought us white rain
Has vanished—the sky is empty;
Our kraal is desolate;
Our calabashes are dry:
And we weep.

F. C. SLATER

The Wood-Gatherers

Oft when the fires of sunset were sinking and dying,
'Mid squatting peaks in the West,
When the skies were freckled with birds swiftly homeward
flying,
And bird-shadows stole from night's nest,
I have watched Xhosa maidens patiently packing and tying
Together the spoils of their quest.

In ochre-dyed vesture that rhymed with the aloes around them,
And the sunbaked soil at their feet,
They burned through the filmy textures of twilight that bound
  them,
Then, their evening labour complete,
With heavy-bunched faggots on heads poised proudly night
  found them
In swift but stately retreat.

'Twixt high kraal and round hut ere-long, in shadowy places,
Leashed flame that struggles shall bite
The fur-padded paws of darkness, while—with their dusky
  faces
In fierce-tongued brilliance alight—
Dark forms shall loom like peaks in the sunset, until all traces
Of fire are lost in night.

F. C. SLATER

Milking Kraal[1]

When stars begin softly to spatter
Milky drops in the bowl overhead;
And the wings of brown bats shear obliquely
The fleece of the dusk;
In the kraal squatting milkers are stitching
Each cow to a pail
With silvery thread.

[1] Kraal: corral, enclosure for cattle or sheep.

Full-bellied cows chew serenely
The cud, and they gulp and they sigh
With contentment; while milkers chant slowly
Songs wordless and strange:
In the distance a veld-ranging jackal
Screws into the silence
His agonized cry.

Now the kindly harvest is gathered,
The milk-pails are carried away;
And sly little herdboys gleefully
Tickle their teeth
With gleanings of milk from reaped udders,
Wisely squeezing last drops
Of delight from spent day.

PERCEVAL GIBBON

Jim

(*An Incident*)

From the Kei to Umzimkulu
　　We chartered to ride,
But before we reached Umtata
　　Jim turned in and died.
　　By Bashee I buried Jim.
Ah! but I was fond of him;
An' but for the niggers grinning,
I'd—yes, I'd have cried.

'Twas a weary trek through Griqualand,
    And me all alone;
Three teams and a dozen niggers
    To boss on my own.
And I felt a need for Jim;
It was just the job for him,
Hazin' the teams and the niggers,
    Hard grit to the bone.

I lost a load at Kokstad:
    An axle fell through;
I hadn't heart to tinker it,
    So pushed on with two.
If I'd only had old Jim!
Axles never broke with him;
But I never could handle waggons
    Like Jim used to do.

I came to Umzimkulu
    With a pain in my head;
I ought to ha' bought med'cine,
    But I liquored instead:
Never used to drink with Jim;
There's a girl that asked for him;
But the jackals root at Bashee—
An' Jim, he's dead!

The Councillor

Old, indeed, as his people go—three score years and ten,
He sat in the dusky council-place and swayed the minds of men;
Chief? Why, no! Nor a Village Head—nor blood nor rank he knew,
But the people hushed to the words he said, the still, hot hours through.

Bleary, battered and broken down—but his law was clean and sound,
Law that had swayed his people's fate full many a cycle round—
Law of the Crop and law of the Chase, and law of the Man and Wife,
The concrete rules of a savage race that govern the Simple Life.

Slow and low were the words he spoke, and each fell trim and plumb,
And the Chief himself leaned forward once as he ravelled out the sum;
Marked each point with a skinny hand, weighed and balanced again,
Quoted the changeless Law of the Land as he made the issue plain.

Passionless as an ice-machine—dreary and dry as dust—
A pitiful, wistful Might-have-been, but sure of the People's trust;

Sure of his logic, sure of the Law, summoned to solve the knot
Of a twopenny-halfpenny case that bore on the right to a
broken pot!

Just the same, in the olden days, they sat in their silent rows,
When men were brought to the judgement-seat to be tried
for the eyes or nose;
Just the same when they burned a man with the partner in
his sin,
Sure of the changeless Law of the Land—bent upon 'rubbing
it in'.

I sat at ease in a patch of shade and thought of the busy Strand,
Of ponderous buildings where men strive to grasp the Law
of the Land,
Of a million lies that obscure the truth, of trickery, sham,
chicane—
There's many a 'tip' to be learned, in sooth, from the Villages
of the Plain!

KINGSLEY FAIRBRIDGE

The Song Maker

Alone in the hot sun,
On the hot sand in the sun,
Alone at the edge of the kraal,
In the dust of the dance-ground
Near the raised tobacco patch;—
The women have gone to the fields,

The children have gone to play,
And the blind Maker of Songs
Sits here, alone, all day.

The dogs sniff'd him and went.
The kraal-rats peer and go,
So very still he sits
Day long, and moon to moon,
His hands slack on the sand;—
And he was just the same,
This maker of tribal songs,
Before the White Men came.

His was the song that woke
The war that brought their power;
The impi went with song—
Came back with song by night,
So many years ago,
With plunder every one;
Leaving among the dead,
Ganero, his only son.

And here, all day, he sits,
On the hot sand in the sun;
The children wonder if he sleeps,
And the flies think him dead,
The dogs smell him and go;—
But to him is bare the lore
Of the Threshing and the Dancing Songs,
And the Chant that leads to War.

BRIAN BROOKE

Smoke of the Camp Fire

'Say, where did you get that spear there?' I asked of the
hunter old,
As we sucked our pipes one ev'ning, when out on the search
for gold.
He slowly removed his briar, and spat in the dancing flame,
Then after a minute he answered, 'You'll reckon my story's
tame;—
But it once belonged to a nigger, whom I saw a "Jumbo" kill,
And somehow I've always kept it, and probably always will.'
Then lapsing again to silence, he reckoned he'd said enough;
He was never a man for talking, was Timothy John McDuff.

But the moon was full above us, and the night was cold and
clear,
And we'd got our Christmas boxes, and opened a case of beer;
We had seen no drink for a quarter, and it happened to loose
his tongue,
And I kept on opening bottles, till I managed to get him
sprung.
Then he started to tell his story, in his usual drawling way:
'Well, it happened like this, my sonny: twelve years ago today
I woke in a darned bad temper, for things had been working
wrong,
—My life had been somewhat reckless, my liver was none
too strong.

'My horse had a cold that morning, and two of my boys
were ill,

31

The sheep which had strayed and wandered are lost in the
bushveld still!

My pistol I found was dirty, and the sight of my rifle bent,
So I flogged it out of my tent-boy, till the most of my rage
was spent.

Then I got on the spoor of a tusker, and told him to keep
behind;
If he wanted no more kiboko, he'd bloomin' well have to
mind.

But he never said "Yea" or "Nay, sir", his face was as hard
as stone,
So he carried my second rifle, and we started away alone.

'It was getting late in the evening, when we sighted the tusker
first;
We'd been on his spoor since sunrise with nothing to quench
our thirst.

And somehow I missed my target and hit him a bit too high;
As he charged away in the brushwood he uttered a piercing
cry.

I was young and daresay foolish, and followed the blood-
stained trail;
I followed for half an hour, till I came on the grand old male.

Then I quickly aimed for his brain-box and drew on him fair
and square,
He moved as I squeezed my trigger,—I missed it by half a
hair.

'It all took place in a second, or possibly rather less;
He charged, and my gun misfired: it usu'lly did in a mess.
So I stood there and watched him coming—you'll find it a
certain rule,

32

When you know that the game is over you'll never be quite
    so cool.
A scurry took place behind me, the sound of a nigger's oath;
I found myself hustled and tumbled down in the undergrowth.
He blazed with my second rifle as he pushed me safe aside,
Then the elephant crashed upon him—and with one long
    moan they died.'

The story was short and finished, I silently sat and smoked;
A fly had got into his bottle and Timothy John had choked.
I felt I should ask him something, to show that I'd heard
    him through,
So I pulled out my plug tobacco and cut off a bit to chew.
Then I said, 'Was the white stuff heavy, and what did they
    weigh the pair?
And what did you do with the nigger? Did you bury or leave
    him there?'
'Say what did I do with the beggar?—Well, what do you
    really think?
He was only a blasted nigger, so shove me another drink.'

ROY CAMPBELL

From *The Flaming Terrapin*

i. Invocation to the African Muse
Far be the bookish Muses! Let them find
Poets more spruce, and with pale fingers wind
The bays in garlands for their northern kind.
My task demands a virgin muse to string
A lyre of savage thunder as I sing.

You who sit brooding on the crags alone,
Nourished on sunlight in a world of stone,
Muse of the Berg, muse of the sounding rocks
Where old Zambezi shakes his hoary locks,
And as they tremble to his awful nod,
Thunder proclaims the presence of a god!
You who have heard with me, when daylight drops,
Those gaunt muezzins of the mountain-tops,
The grey baboons, salute the rising moon
And watched with me the long horizons swoon
In twilight, when the lorn hyaena's strain
Reared to the clouds its lonely tower of pain.
Now while across the night with dismal hum
The hurricanes, your meistersingers, come,
Choose me some lonely hill-top in the range
To be my Helicon, and let me change
This too-frequented Hippocrene for one
That thunders flashing to my native sun
Or in the night hushes his waves to hear
How, armed and crested with a sable plume,
Like a dark cloud, clashing a ghostly spear,
The shade of Tchaka strides across the gloom.
Write what I sing in red corroding flame,
Let it be hurled in thunder on the dark,
And as the vast earth trembles through its frame,
Salute with me the advent of the Ark!

ii. *The Fall of Satan*

Like a stone toppled from an endless hill,
Compelled as by some fierce insensate·will,
Colliding and rebounding from the crags,
Sheer through the deep he tore his whistling rags.
And while through those grim vaults and starless gaps

He rumbled in his hideous collapse,
The damned, each like a grey hook-tailed baboon,
Grown blind with yearning on the fruitless moon,
Hearing his fall, stole forth in rustling troops,
Cramned the cold ledges of the cliff that stoops
Bowed o'er the pit, and there with groping sight
Followed his sinking phantom through the night.
For weary months from cliff to crag he fell,
Until at last the grim recess of Hell,
Stunned by his fall, gave forth a horrid groan
From all its jolted battlements of stone.
And as he dragged his body from the flood,
Pocking deep craters in the sucking mud,
The Dead, like weary snipe, rising on high,
Whined through the gusty pallor of the sky,
And left him there, rending the night with moans,
To nurse the mangled relics of his bones.

iii. Noah

High on the top of Ararat alone
Old Noah stood: beneath him faintly blown,
Great aasvogels, like beetles on a pond,
Veered in slow circles o'er the gulf beyond.
The dusk came on: faint shades began to streak
Across the dim cathedral of the peak,
And from his craggy pulpit, the baboon
Rose on the skyline, mitred with the moon.
Over far Edens waved the golden lights
Trailing their gorgeous fringes o'er the heights.
Under the dying splendours of the day,
Rolling around him from his frosty throne,
Ridged with red skies, his mighty kingdom lay
Stretching to heaven. Zone on sweeping zone,

Huge circles outward swirled without a bound,
The world's immense horizons ringed him round,
Receding, merging on until the whole
Creation on the pivot of his soul
Seemed to be wheeling: star on lonely star
Haloed him with its orbit from afar.
He was the axle of the wheel, the pole
Round which the galaxies and systems roll,
And from his being, making months and years
Issued the vast momentum of the spheres.
Those mighty rings seemed but the ripples flung
From his great soul in lofty triumph swung,
An Aphrodite rising from the deep
Of old despairs. Matter's forlorn desire,
Through souls of men, in mighty deeds to leap,
Rose in his soul and crowned itself with fire.
And as the Night, serene and chaste and cold,
Down the faint air on starry pinions rolled,
Loud shouts of triumph through the valleys ran,
And Noah turned to watch, far in the west,
The sun's great phoenix fold her scarlet fan
And sink in ruin from the snowy crest.
There as amid the growing shades he stood
Facing alone the sky's vast solitude,
That space, which gods and demons fear to scan,
Smiled on the proud irreverence of Man.

ROY CAMPBELL

The Serf

His naked skin clothed in the torrid mist
That puffs in smoke around the patient hooves,
The ploughman drives, a slow somnambulist,
And through the green his crimson furrow grooves.
His heart, more deeply than he wounds the plain,
Long by the rasping share of insult torn,
Red clod, to which the war-cry once was rain
And tribal spears the fatal sheaves of corn,
Lies fallow now. But as the turf divides
I see in the slow progress of his strides
Over the toppled clods and falling flowers,
The timeless, surly patience of the serf
That moves the nearest to the naked earth
And ploughs down palaces, and thrones, and towers.

ROY CAMPBELL

The Zulu Girl

To F. C. Slater

When in the sun the hot red acres smoulder,
Down where the sweating gang its labour plies,
A girl flings down her hoe, and from her shoulder
Unslings her child tormented by the flies.

She takes him to a ring of shadow pooled
By thorn-trees: purpled with the blood of ticks,

37

While her sharp nails, in slow caresses ruled,
Prowl through his hair with sharp electric clicks,

His sleepy mouth plugged by the heavy nipple,
Tugs like a puppy, grunting as he feeds:
Through his frail nerves her own deep languors ripple
Like a broad river sighing through its reeds.

Yet in that drowsy stream his flesh imbibes
An old unquenched unsmotherable heat—
The curbed ferocity of beaten tribes,
The sullen dignity of their defeat.

Her body looms above him like a hill
Within whose shade a village lies at rest,
Or the first cloud so terrible and still
That bears the coming harvest in its breast.

ROY CAMPBELL

The Zebras

To Chips Rafferty
From the dark woods that breathe of fallen showers,
Harnessed with level rays in golden reins,
The zebras draw the dawn across the plains
Wading knee-deep among the scarlet flowers.
The sunlight, zithering their flanks with fire,
Flashes between the shadows as they pass
Barred with electric tremors through the grass
Like wind along the gold strings of a lyre.

Into the flushed air snorting rosy plumes
That smoulder round their feet in drifting fumes,
With dove-like voices call the distant fillies,
While round the herds the stallion wheels his flight,
Engine of beauty volted with delight,
To roll his mare among the trampled lilies.

ROY CAMPBELL

From: *The Wayzgoose*[1]

Attend my fable if your ears be clean,
In fair Banana Land we lay our scene—
South Africa, renowned both far and wide
For politics and little else beside:
Where, having torn the land with shot and shell,
Our sturdy pioneers as farmers dwell,
And, 'twixt the hours of strenuous sleep, relax
To shear the fleeces or to fleece the blacks:
Where every year a fruitful increase bears
Of pumpkins, sheep, and millionaires—
A clime so prosperous both to men and kine
That which were which a sage could scarce define;[2]
Where fat white sheep upon the mountains bleat
And fatter politicians in the street;
Where lemons hang like yellow moons ashine
And grapes the size of apples load the vine;

[1] 'This phenomenon occurs annually in S.A. It appears to be a vast corroboree of journalists, and to judge from their own reports of it, it combines the functions of a bunfight, an Eisteddfod and an Olympic contest.' (Campbell's note.)

[2] Example: 'Wanted: a good short-horn typist.' S.A. newspaper.

Where apples to the weight of pumpkins go
And donkeys to the height of statesmen grow,
Where trouts the size of salmon throng the creeks
And worms the size of magistrates—the beaks;
Where the precocious tadpole, from his bog
Becomes a journalist ere half a frog;
Where every shrimp his proud career may carve
And only brain and muscle have to starve.
The 'garden colony' they call our land,
And surely for a garden it was planned:
What apter phrase with such a place could cope
Where vegetation has so fine a scope,
Where *weeds* in such variety are found
And all the rarest *parasites* abound,
Where pumpkins to professors are promoted
And turnips into Parliament are voted?

ROY CAMPBELL

On Some South African Novelists

You praise the firm restraint with which they write—
I'm with you there, of course:
They use the snaffle and the curb all right,
But where's the bloody horse?

ROY CAMPBELL

On the Same

Far from the vulgar haunts of men
Each sits in her 'successful room',
Housekeeping with her fountain pen
And writing novels with her broom.

ROY CAMPBELL

From *A Veld Eclogue: The Pioneers*

. . . But 'nameless somethings' and 'unbounded spaces'
Are still the heritage of 'younger races'—
At least our novelists will have it so,
And, reader, who are we to tell them, 'No!'
We, who have never heard the 'call', or felt
The witching whatdyecallum of the veld?
As for that 'nameless something', it was there
Plain as the grime upon their ragged hair—
Bolitho[1] calls it an 'inspired alertness'
And so it seemed (in spite of their inertness)—
A worried look, as if they half-expected
Something to happen, or half-recollected
Anything having happened there at all
Since old Oom Jaapie's heifer calved last fall.

[1] Hector, not William. Prolific and popular interpreter of the 'New Earth', the 'Open Spaces', etc., to which he even relates the present writer's poems. Accounting for the mental and physical 'superiority' of the Colonial to the European, B. writes: ' "It's the distance that does it," said my millionaire, looking at me with his rather fine head chiselled on a background of cream madonna-lilies, "it's the distance that does it." '

As for the 'boundless spaces'—wild and free
They stretched around as far as eye could see,
Which, though not very far, was yet enough
To show a tree, four houses, and a bluff.
Geographers, who say the world's a sphere,
Are either ignorant, or mazed with beer,
Or liars—or have never read two pages
Of any of our novelists or sages
Who tell us plainly that the world's more wide
On the colonial than the other side,
That states and kingdoms are less vast and grand
Than ranches, farms and mealie-planted land,
And that wherever on the world's bald head
A province or protectorate is spread
The place straightway to vast proportions jumps
As with the goitre or a dose of mumps—
So that in shape our cosmos should compare
Less with an apple than a warty pear.
For all our scenery's in grander style
And there are far more furlongs to the mile
In Africa than Europe—though, no doubt
None but colonials have found this out.
For though our Drakensberg's most lofty scalps
Would scarcely reach the waist-line of the Alps,
Though Winterberg, besides the Pyrenees,
Would scarcely reach on tip-toe to their knees,
Nobody can deny that our hills rise
Far more majestically—for their size!
I mean that there is something grander, yes,
About the veld, than I can well express,
Something more vast—perhaps I don't mean that—
Something more round, and square, and steep, and flat—
No, well, perhaps it's not quite that I mean,

But something, rather, half-way in between,
Something more 'nameless'—That's the very word!
Something that can't be felt, or seen, or heard,
Or even thought—a kind of mental mist
That doesn't either matter or exist
But without which it would go very hard
With many a local novelist and bard—
Being the only trick they've ever done,
To bring in local colour where there's none:
And if I introduce the system too,
Blame only the traditions I pursue.

ROY CAMPBELL

Rounding the Cape

The low sun whitens on the flying squalls,
Against the cliffs the long grey surge is rolled
Where Adamastor[1] from his marble halls
Threatens the sons of Lusus as of old.

Faint on the glare uptowers the dauntless form,
Into whose shade abysmal as we draw,
Down on our decks, from far above the storm,
Grin the stark ridges of his broken jaw.

[1] Adamastor: 'The spirit of the Cape whose apparition and prophecy form one of the finest passages in *The Lusiads* of Camoens' (Roy Campbell). Adamastor hates the intrusion of his immemorial privacy, and threatens the venturing Sons of Lusus with disaster and shipwreck. His curse was so effective that no European settlement was attempted at the Cape for a century and a half after its discovery. He is one of the giant sons of earth, primitive, passionate, stupid, who, frustrated in his love for Thetis, goes into a remote, sulky exile, having realized that 'mere strength is of no avail against the heavens'. See Canto Five, *The Lusiads*, trans. William C. Atkinson (Penguin Classics).

43

Across his back, unheeded, we have broken
Whole forests: heedless of the blood we've spilled,
In thunder still his prophecies are spoken,
In silence, by the centuries, fulfilled.

Farewell, terrific shade! though I go free
Still of the powers of darkness art thou Lord,
I watch the phantom sinking in the sea
Of all that I have hated or adored.

The prow glides smoothly on through seas quiescent:
But where the last point sinks into the deep,
The land lies dark beneath the rising crescent,
And Night, the Negro, murmurs in his sleep.

ROY CAMPBELL

The Sling

Guarding the cattle on my native hill
This was my talisman. Its charm was known
High in the blue and aquiline ozone,
And by my tireless armourer, the rill,
Smoothing his pellets to my hand or eye:
And how its meteors sang into the sky
The eagles of the Berg[1] remember still.

I wore this herdsman's bracelet all day long:
To me it meant 'To-morrow' and 'Perhaps',
The insults of Goliath, his collapse,

[1] Berg: mountain; here, the Drakensberg.

Much fighting, and (who knows?) a life of song.
So fine a jewel at his wrist to swing
(For it was Chance) has seldom graced a king—
As I have dangled on a rawhide thong.

It spelt me luck in every polished stone
That to its mark, or thereabouts, had won:
For it had been to a poor herdsman's son
A stirrup once, to vault into a throne
And ride a nation over its despair;
To me, it seemed an amulet of prayer,
Remembering David and the warrior Joan.

I thought of the incendiary hope
Such herdsmen brought to cities from the hills,
Taught by the rash example of the rills,
Leaping in fire, to rush the headlong slope,
To gather impetus for height that's lost,
And hurtle through, regardless of the cost,
Where cunning or precaution have no scope.

When I have felt the whiff of madness' wing,
And rioted in barrios[1] of shame,
Where all they gave me was a thirsty flame,
To burn my lips, that could no longer sing—
Around my fevered pulse to cool the flame,
There ghosted at my wrist an airy sling
And drew me to a garden, or a spring.

My link, in its long absence, with delight:
My handcuff (if I looked upon a knife)
That chained me to the miracle of life

[1] Barrio: city quarters (Sp.).

45

Through a long frost and winter of the sprite:
And ready, at most need, to arm my prayer,
As once, when cries and feathers filled the air,
It saved a silver egret from a kite.

When stranded on these unfamiliar feet
Without a horse, and in the Stranger's land,
Like any tamest Redneck to your hand,
I shuffled with the Charlies in the street
Forgetting I was born a Centaur's foal;
When like the rest, I would have sawn my soul
Short at the waist, where man and mount should meet—

Its tightened thong would jerk me to control,
And never let the solar memory set
Of those blue highlands which are Eden yet
For all the rage of dynamite or coal—
Whose sunrise is the vision that I see then,
That, hurled like Bruce's heart amongst the heathen,
Leads on our White Commando to its goal!

Where none break ranks though down the whole race treks,
It taught me how to separate, and choose;
The uniform they ordered, to refuse—
The hornrimmed eyes, the ringworm round their necks;
And, when the Prince of herdsmen rode on high,
To rope those hikers with that bolshie tie,
To save my scruff, and see without the specs:—

Choosing my pebbles (to distinguish, free)
I had dispensed with numbers; finding how,
Since Space was always Here as Time was Now,
Extent of either means a Fig to me;

To the whole field I can prefer a flower
And know that States are foundered by an hour
While centuries may groan to fell a tree.

By its cool guidance I unread my books
And learned, in spite of theories and charts,
Things have a nearer meaning to their looks
Than to their dead analyses in parts;
And how (for all the outfit be antique)
Our light is in our heads; and we can seek
The clearest information in our hearts.

It taught me to inflict or suffer pain:
That my worst fortune was to serve me right,
And though it be the fashion to complain,
Self-pity is the ordure of the sprite,
But faith its ichor; and though in my course,
A rival knot the grass to spill my horse,
That trusting all to luck is half the fight.

It taught me that the world is not for Use;
But is, to each, the fruit of his desire,
From whose superb Grenade to swill the juice,
Some thaw its rosy frost into a fire—
Leaving the husks they most expect to find
To those insisting on the horny rind;
For it rewards as we to it aspire.

So ripe a fruit, so ruddy, and so real!—
To-night it bleeds, as when in days gone by
(Aldebaran a rowel at my heel)
I rounded up the cattle on the sky
Against the Berg's Toledo-steepled walls—

As now, upon the mesas of Castile
Beside the city that it most recalls.

For him whose teeth can crack the bitter rind—
Still to his past the future will reply,
And build a sacred city in his mind
With singing towers to thunder in the wind:
To light his life will shine the herdsman King
Who whirls our great Pomegranate in his sling
To herd the other planets through the sky.

Slung at his wrist will hang the phantom stress
Of David's stone—to weigh that all is right;
Even to daunt him should the weak unite
On one Goliath, he'll accept and bless,
Whose home's the Earth, and Everywhere his bed
A sheepskin saddle to his seat or head,
And Here and Now his permanent address.

ROY CAMPBELL

Luis de Camoes

Camoes, alone of all the lyric race,
Born in the black aurora of disaster,
Can look a common soldier in the face:
I find a comrade where I sought a master:
For daily, while the stinking crocodiles
Glide from the mangroves on the swampy shore,
He shares my awning on the dhow, he smiles,

And tells me that he lived it all before.
Through fire and shipwreck, pestilence and loss,
Led by the ignis fatuus of duty
To a dog's death—yet of his sorrows king—
He shouldered high his voluntary Cross,
Wrestled his hardships into forms of beauty,
And taught his gorgon destinies to sing.

ROY CAMPBELL

Dreaming Spires

Through villages of yelping tykes
With skulls on totem-poles, and wogs
Exclaiming at our motor bikes
With more amazement than their dogs:

Respiring fumes of pure phlogiston
On hardware broncos, half-machine,
With arteries pulsing to the piston
And hearts inducting gasoline;

Buckjumping over ruts and boulders,
The Centaurs of an age of steel
Engrafted all save head and shoulders
Into the horsepower of the wheel—

We roared into the open country,
Scattering vultures, kites, and crows;
All Nature scolding our effrontery
In raucous agitation rose.

Zoology went raving stark
To meet us on the open track—
The whole riff-raff of Noah's Ark
With which the wilderness was black.

With kicks and whinnies, bucks and snorts,
Their circuses stampeded by:
A herd of wildebeest cavorts,
And somersaults against the sky:

Across the stripes of zebras sailing,
The eyesight rattles like a cane
That's rattled down an area-railing
Until it blurs upon the brain:

The lions flee with standing hackles,
Leaving their feast before they've dined:
Their funeral poultry flaps and cackles
To share the breeze they feel behind.

Both wart- and road-hog vie together,
As they and we, petarding smoke,
Belly to earth and hell for leather,
In fumes of dust and petrol choke.

We catch the madness they have caught,
Stand on the footrests, and guffaw—
Till shadowed by a looming thought
And visited with sudden awe,

We close our throttles, clench the curb,
And hush the rumble of our tyres,
Abashed and fearful to disturb
The City of the Dreaming Spires—

The City of Giraffes!—a People
Who live between the earth and skies,
Each in his lone religious steeple,
Keeping a light-house with his eyes:

Each his own stairway, tower, and stylite,
Ascending on his saintly way
Up rungs of gold into the twilight
And leafy ladders to the day:

Chimneys of silence! at whose summit,
Like storks, the daydreams love to nest;
The Earth, descending like a plummet
Into the oceans of unrest,

They can ignore—whose nearer neighbour
The sun is, with the stars and moon
That on their hides, with learned labour,
Tattooed the hieroglyphic rune.

Muezzins that from airy pylons
Peer out above the golden trees
Where the mimosas fleece the silence
Or slumber on the drone of bees:

Nought of this earth they see but flowers
Quilting a carpet to the sky
To where some pensive crony towers
Or Kilimanjaro takes the eye.

Their baser passions fast on greens
Where, never to intrude or push,
Their bodies live like submarines,
Far down beneath them, in the bush.

Around their head the solar glories,
With their terrestrial sisters fly—
Rollers, and orioles, and lories,
And trogons of the evening sky.

Their bloodstream with a yeasty leaven
Exalts them to the stars above,
As we are raised, though not to heaven,
By drink—or when we fall in love.

By many a dismal crash and wreck
Our dreams are weaned of aviation,
But these have beaten (by a neck!)
The steepest laws of gravitation.

Some animals have all the luck,
Who hurl their breed in nature's throat—
Out of a gumtree by a buck,
Or escalator—by a goat!

When I have worked my ticket, pension,
And whatsoever I can bum,
To colonise the fourth dimension,
With my Beloved, I may come,

And buy a pair of stilts for both,
And hire a periscope for two,
To vegetate in towering sloth
Out here amongst these chosen few . . .

Or so my fancies seemed to sing
To see, across the gulf of years,
The soldiers of a reigning King
Confront those ghostly halberdiers.

But someone kicks his starter back:
Anachronism cocks its ears.
Like Beefeaters who've got the sack
With their own heads upon their spears;

Like Leftwing Poets at the hint
Of work, or danger, or the blitz,
Or when they catch the deadly glint
Of satire, swordplay of the wits,—

Into the dusk of leafy oceans
They fade away with phantom tread;
And changing gears, reversing notions,
The road to Moshi roars ahead.

WILLIAM PLOMER

The Scorpion

Limpopo and Tugela churned
In flood for brown and angry miles
Melons, maize, domestic thatch,
The trunks of trees and crocodiles;

The swollen estuaries were thick
With flotsam, in the sun one saw
The corpse of a young negress bruised
By rocks, and rolling on the shore,

Pushed by the waves of morning, rolled
Impersonally among shells,
With lolling breasts and bleeding eyes,
And round her neck were beads and bells.

That was the Africa we knew,
Where, wandering alone,
We saw, heraldic in the heat,
A scorpion on a stone.

WILLIAM PLOMER

Namaqualand after Rain

Again the veld revives,
Imbued with lyric rains,
And sap re-sweetening dry stalks
Perfumes the quickening plains;

Small roots explode in strings of stars,
Each bulb gives up its dream,
Honey drips from orchid throats,
Jewels each raceme;

The desert sighs at dawn—
As in another hemisphere
The temple lotus breaks her buds
On the attentive air—

A frou-frou of new flowers,
Puff of unruffling petals,
While rods of sunlight strike pure streams
From rocks beveined with metals;

Far in the gaunt karroo
That winter dearth denudes,
Ironstone caves give back the burr
Of lambs in multitudes;

Grass waves again where drought
Bleached every upland kraal,
A peach-tree shoots along the wind
Pink volleys through a broken wall,

And willows growing round the dam
May now be seen
With all their traceries of twigs
Just hesitating to be green,

Soon to be hung with colonies
All swaying with the leaves
Of pendent wicker love-nests
The pretty loxia weaves.

WILLIAM PLOMER

The Ruined Farm

A peaceful, archangelic sun
Sank low, grew larger to the sight,
And drew across each huge ravine
The huger curtains of the night;

Silence within the roofless house
Undid her hair and shook it free,
The footpad jackal passed her there,
And bats flew round the cactus-tree;

Each quiet afternoon was bitter,
Was overcharged with warning,
And Silence waited where the snake lay coiled
And mocked at each mild, bright morning.

WILLIAM PLOMER

The Death of a Zulu

The weather is mild
At the house of one of the dead.
There is fruit in the hands of his child
With flowers on its head.

Smoke rises up from the floor,
And the hands of a ghost
(No shadow darkens the door)
Caress the door-post.

Inside sits the wife, frantic, forsaken,
Too wild to weep;
Food lies uncooked at her feet, and is taken
By venturing fowls:
Outside, the dogs were asleep,
But they waken,
And one of them howls;
And Echo replies.

At last, with a sudden fear shaken,
The little child cries.

The Boer War

The whip-crack of a Union Jack
In a stiff breeze (the ship will roll),
Deft abracadabra drums
Enchant the patriotic soul—

A grandsire in St. James's Street
Sat at the window of his club,
His second son, shot through the throat,
Slid backwards down a slope of scrub,

Gargled his last breaths, one by one by one,
In too much blood, too good to spill,
Died difficultly, drop by drop by drop—
'By your son's courage, sir, we took the hill.'

The Pioneers:
Or, Twenty Years After

The street, the store, the station, especially the bar,
Show what the fathers of this tin-town hamlet are:
Moustaches waxed, these mammoths lean on counters,
Old rotting whales ashore and thick with flies,
Their blubber proof to bullets and to kicks,
Fill up their lungs with beer and blow out spouts of lies,
Tales of rebellions, cannons and encounters,
Before their brains dried up in nineteen-six.

The Explorer

Romantic subject of the Great White Queen,
See him advancing, whiskered and serene,
With helmet, spectacles, and flask of brandy,
(That useful stimulant, he always keeps it handy),
Unmoved by cannibals, indifferent to disease,
His black frock-coat rocks sadly in the tropic breeze.

He never shows emotion, least of all surprise.
Here nothing meets his fat and hopeful eyes
But big game, small game, fur and fin and feather,
And now he dreams of daisies, Scotland and the Flag,
The nimble corncrake in his native heather,
The handy corkscrew in his leather bag.

WILLIAM PLOMER

Johannesburg

Along the Rand in eighty-five
Fortunes were founded overnight,
And mansions rose among the rocks
To blaze with girls and light;

In champagne baths men sluiced their skins
Grimy with auriferous dust,
Then oiled and scented, fought to enjoy
What young men must;

Took opportunities to cheat,
Or meet the most expensive whore,
And conjured up with cards and dice,
New orgies from new veins of ore;

Greybeards who now look back
To the old days
Find little in their past to blame
And much to praise—

Riding bareback under stars
As lordly anarchs of the veld,
Venison feasts and tribal wars
Free cruelty and a cartridge belt;

Pioneers, O pioneers,
Grey pillars of a Christian State,
Respectability has turned
Swashbuckler prim and scamp sedate;

Prospecting in the brain's recesses
Seek now the nuggets of your prime,
And sift the gold dust of your dreams
From drifted sands of time.

WILLIAM PLOMER

The Victoria Falls

These are the Victoria Falls, whose noisy gushing
Attracts a noisy and a gushing crowd;
They rush from every country in the world to gape
At this cascade that is the usual shape.

Over the brink a lot of water leaps
By force of gravity, and many a tourist peeps
Into the gulf to see a natural law fulfilled
And quantities of water that never stop being spilled.

These are the Victoria Falls, the brightest trinket
In the globe-trotter's box of well-worn curios:
If they want water, good God, let them drink it!
If they want falls, we'll knock them down—here goes!

Why do you come, I wonder, all this weary way?
Is it because you like to smile and say,
'When we were at the Falls the other day——'?
Is it because you like to see the spray?

Is it because you like to feel how far
It is from Boston to these falls of the Zambesi
Which must be falling still? Or do you feel uneasy
Until you know how like their photograph they are?

A female tourist raves, 'We're keen as keen
On Africa! It's dusty—but, my dears, the *sun*!
I had a list of all the things we've seen,
I can't remember half the things we've done!

The Kaffirs? Well, they're black, and live in such quaint
    kraals.
They're dusty, too! The great thing is to see the Falls,
The rainbows, and the Rain Forest, where we all wore mack-
    intoshes,
Admired the ferns, and were so glad we'd all brought our
    galoshes
(The water spirits leered at her, the lurking *tokoloshes*).

'My dear, the spray! the noise! the view! the beautiful hotel!
Electric light in every room, and an electric bell!
So clean and comfortable, and they looked after us so well!'

Harsh and insistent, a guide-book on a gramophone,
She will not go away. . . . Ach, I long to be alone
With a guide-book to the gentle Falls of Silence,
The Temple of Reticence on the Tranquil Islands,
Where no sound enters, whence no sound goes out,
And waterfalls
        Fall quietly
                As tea falls
                        From a spout.

WILLIAM PLOMER

The Devil-Dancers

In shantung suits we whites are cool,
Glasses and helmets censoring the glare;
Fever has made our anxious faces pale,
We stoop a little from the load we bear;

61

Grouped in the shadow of the compound wall
We get our cameras ready, sitting pensive;
Keeping our distance and our dignity
We talk and smile, though slightly apprehensive.

The heat strikes upward from the ground,
The ground the natives harden with their feet,
The flag is drooping on its bamboo pole,
The middle distance wavers in the heat.

Naked or gaudy, all agog the crowd
Buzzes and glistens in the sun; the sight
Dazzles the retina; we remark the smell,
The drums beginning, and the vibrant light.

Now the edge of the jungle rustles. In a hush
The crowd parts. Nothing happens. Then
The dancers totter adroitly out on stilts,
Weirdly advancing, twice as high as men.

Sure as fate, strange as the mantis, cruel
As vengeance in a dream, four bodies hung
In cloaks of rasping grasses, turning
Their tiny heads, the masks besmeared with dung;

Each mops and mows, uttering no sound,
Each stately, awkward, giant marionette,
Each printed shadow frightful on the ground
Moving in small distorted silhouette;

The fretful pipes and thinly-crying strings,
The mounting expectation of the drums
Excite the nerves, and stretch the muscles taut
Against the climax—but it never comes;

It never comes because the dance must end
And very soon the dancers will be dead;
We leave by air to-morrow; how
Can ever these messages by us be read?

These bodies hung with viscera and horns
Move with an incomparable lightness,
And through the masks that run with bullocks' blood
Quick eyes look out, dots of fanatic brightness.

Within the mask the face, and moulded
(As mask to face) within the face the ghost,
As in its chrysalis-case the foetus folded
Of leaf-light butterfly. What matters most

When it comes out and we admire its wings
Is to remember where its life began:
Let us take care—that flake of flame may be
The butterfly whose bite can kill a man.

WILLIAM PLOMER

A Traveller's Tale

'. . . *des horizons défaits qui se refont plus loin*'

We came that way by choice,
Preferred
Desert and altitude.
That was the way we chose,
We should choose it again.

We should come that way again
Though not the men we were.
Mountain fever has left us thin,
We still see snow, the wind
That drove the grit against the skin
Has left our faces scarred,
Our cheeks have fallen in,
Our foreheads wear the anxious lines
That acid doubt takes time to groove,
But why complain?

We are not without reward
For our senses were enriched
By the difficult and rare,
The rare and strange,
The little known, the chanced upon,
Moments worth waiting for
And slowly won by weeks of care,
Moments when hope
Fell open like a shell,
And showed the pearl,
And the pearl lay in the palm.

And why did we start out?
We were impelled
To choose the way we came.
And what have we to show but scars?
Not for us to tell
Everything we know.

Sometimes in twos or threes,
But oftener one by one,
We made our way along

And met from time to time
Comparing notes and mapping routes.
We climbed for days towards the sky
But only came on dry plateaux
With various views
Of heights too huge to climb,
The massif, where a hooded storm
Darkens the peaks day in, day out,
But keeps the foothills green.

We cannot be too grateful
To the desert tribes,
The nomads who for shawls or beads
Helped us along,
But best of all we saw
Some pure-bred people of those parts,
Rare types, a race who act
Not for applause or momentary effect,
Who make the best of what they find
But most respect
What might exist.

All their native music comes
From instruments with just one string
Accompanied by drums,
We heard them sing
And saw them dance,
They only moved their heads and arms
But a nod of theirs means more
Than the march of crowds means here.

We heard the native names of towns
Sounding like stones let fall in pools
Or rocks rebounding between waterfalls

At daybreak into deep ravines,
But saw no towns,
Perhaps there are no towns,
Perhaps their towns
Are legends like their lives.

We know their eyes reflect
Perfections that outdo
What we conceive
At moments when the pearl
Lies perfect in the palm.
No, not the men we were
Before we came that way,
Anonymous and proud
We wear our scars with joy,
Yes, we who spent ourselves
To take a chosen way.

WILLIAM PLOMER

A Transvaal Morning

A sudden waking when a saffron glare
Suffused the room, and sharper than a quince
Two bird-notes penetrated there
Piercing the cloistral deep veranda twice.

The stranger started up to face
The sulphur sky of Africa, an infinite
False peace, the trees in that dry place
Like painted bones, their stillness like a threat.

Shoulders of quartz protruded from the hill
Like sculpture half unearthed; red dust,
Impalpable as cinnamon softly sifted, filled
With heaped-up silence rift and rut.

Again those two keen bird-notes! And the pert
Utterer, a moss-green thrush, was there
In the veranda-cave, alert,
About to flit into the breathless air.

The strangeness plucked the stranger like a string.
'They say this constant sun outstares the mind,
Here in this region of the fang, the sting,
And dulls the eye to what is most defined.

'A wild bird's eye on the *qui vive*
Perhaps makes vagueness clear and staleness new;
If undeceived one might not then deceive;
Let me', he thought, 'attain the bird's-eye view.'

ALAN PATON

Sanna[1]

The village lies in Sabbath heat
The dog lies in the sun
But stern and strict the elders go
They pass me one by one.

[1] A common name among African or Coloured servants.

The alien traffic swirls and blows
The dust about the street
But stern and strict the elders go
In any dust or heat.

And careless words are spoken
By idlers of the place
But stern and strict the elders go
To hear the words of grace.

And stern and strict the sabbath clothes
And stern the eyes above
And stern and strict the elders go
To hear the words of love.

And Sanna follows all demure
And plays her little part
The child of love moves in her womb
And terror in her heart.

ALAN PATON

The Discardment

We gave her a discardment
A trifle, a thing no longer to be worn,
Its purpose served, its life done.
She put it on with exclamations,
Her eyes shone, she called and cried,

The great bulk of her pirouetted
She danced and mimed, sang snatches of a song.
She called out blessings in her native tongue
Called to her fellow-servants
To strangers and to passers-by
To all the continent of Africa
To see this wonder, to participate
In this intolerable joy.

And so for nothing
Is purchased loyalty and trust
And the unquestioning obedience
Of the earth's most rare simplicity.
So for nothing
The destruction of a world.

ALAN PATON

Samuel

The black boy rose from his bed
And came to me willingly
And master, master, he said
Why did you call for me?

But I told him I called no word
And he said to me sheepishly
I must have dreamt that I heard
The master calling me.

And again he rose from his bed
And came to me willingly
And master, master, he said
Why did you call for me?

But I told him I called no word
And he said to me with shame
I dreamt again that I heard
The master calling my name.

And yet again from his bed
He came to me willingly
And master, master, he said
Why did you call for me?

Now God is great I know
But He can't quite understand
Or why should He summon so
Black boys in a white man's land?

I did not call, I said,
And I have no mind to call
For God's sake go to your bed
And answer no more at all.

ALAN PATON

To a Small Boy who Died at Diepkloof Reformatory

Small offender, small innocent child
With no conception or comprehension
Of the vast machinery set in motion
By your trivial transgression,
Of the great forces of authority,
Of judges, magistrates, and lawyers,
Psychologists, psychiatrists, and doctors,
Principals, police, and sociologists,
Kept moving and alive by your delinquency,
This day, and under the shining sun
Do I commit your body to the earth
Oh child, oh lost and lonely one.

Clerks are moved to action by your dying;
Your documents, all neatly put together,
Are transferred from the living to the dead,
Here is the document of birth
Saying that you were born and where and when,
But giving no hint of joy or sorrow,
Or if the sun shone, or if the rain was falling,
Or what bird flew singing over the roof
Where your mother travailed. And here your name
Meaning in white man's tongue, he is arrived,
But to what end or purpose is not said.

Here is the last certificate of Death;
Forestalling authority he sets you free,

You that did once arrive have now departed
And are enfolded in the sole embrace
Of kindness that earth ever gave to you.
So negligent in life, in death belatedly
She pours her generous abundance on you
And rains her bounty on the quivering wood
And swaddles you about, where neither hail nor tempest,
Neither wind nor snow nor any heat of sun
Shall now offend you, and the thin cold spears
Of the highveld rain that once so pierced you
In falling on your grave shall press you closer
To the deep repentant heart.

Here is the warrant of committal,
For this offence, oh small and lonely one,
For this offence in whose commission
Millions of men are in complicity
You are committed. So do I commit you,
Your frail body to the waiting ground,
Your dust to the dust of the veld,—
Fly home-bound soul to the great Judge-President
Who unencumbered by the pressing need
To give society protection, may pass on you
The sentence of the indeterminate compassion.

H. C. BOSMAN

The Poet

I don't say that the Fates were actuated
By any deliberate malice: I only say

That when they bestowed on me the gifts they did
They were careless. Why should I be fated
To bear the whole moon? Why could they not weigh
Out so much? Instead of a sky panoplied
With flighted images I'd sooner have
A mealie-field to gaze on: I would try
To keep the growing earth within the sound
Of my blood. The Fates were careless when they gave
Me these banished things in superfluity—
Lost facts brooding like temples instead of ground
For seed and harvest. I would never seek at all
The poppied riot of imaginings
With summer dreams trampled under the wind's horses
And sorrow masked for a last carnival.
I want the sullied soil, not these fine things
That have their ends in water-lights, their sources
In old imperial desolations. Wings
    Are angel's wear, not Jacob's. Why should I
    Blonde-pinion accoutremented be
    In list in this most awful rivalry?

H. C. BOSMAN

Seed

The farmer ploughs into the ground
More than the wheat-seed strewn on the ground
The farmer ploughs into the ground
The plough and the oxen and his body
He ploughs into the ground the farmstead and the cattle

73

And the pigs and the poultry and the kitchen utensils
And the afternoon sunlight shining into the window panes of
    the voorhuis[1]
And the light entangled in the eyes of his children
He ploughs into the ground his wife's brown body
And the windmill above the borehole
And the borehole and the wind driving the windmill.
The farmer ploughs the blue clouds into the ground;
And as a tribute to the holocaust of the ploughshare—
To the sowing that was the parting of the Juggernaut—
The earth renders the farmer in due season
Corn.

H. C. BOSMAN

From *The Luck in the Square Stone*

I

At the safari's end a porter
Sorrows in his loins for the load that has been shifted
From his shoulders, yearning
Because the journeying
On the young road was shorter;
And in his brown palm the clean-sifted
Silver feels like Judas-pieces, a blood guerdon
For his betrayal of the burden
Long in love-hate carried, sudden lifted.
The same heart burns
For ermine, pearls and gold,
That yearns
For rags in the cold.

[1] Voorhuis: living room (Afrikaans).

It is only when love comes
That people grow afraid:
In the tribal dance the tom-toms
Are both man and maid.
It is only when love comes
That things are no more said,
And the wood and the skin of the tribal drums
Speak for both man and maid.

H. C. BOSMAN

Recovery from Mental Illness

I had been ill; and when I saw
The world again without a flaw—

A pigeon tumbling in blue air,
A yellow leaf in the winter bare,

A gemmed ring on a maiden's finger—
I was glad my thoughts did not linger

Too long within the laid-out pleasaunce
Of my body's convalescence,

But that they came in-doors quite soon
And opened a curtain to the moon.

I lay with the full moon on my bed,
But a crescent moon shone in my head.

The straighter that the pavements tend
The crookeder the people bend.

The straight sidewalks of Eloff Street[1]
Were never made for human feet

For we are born to greener chains
Than we well know: our grassy brains
Closer to bees and suns and rains.

As calm as the outward lunar ray,
So wild is the inward moon alway.

R. N. CURREY

From *Man's Roots*

Man's roots are not in earth; while trees and flowers
Stand in one place, the intimate atmospheres
Blown through their leaves, and the remoter spheres
Of space whirled round them every twenty-four hours,

Even the peasant, who, in growing showers,
Stands solid in his furrow, at times tears
His boots from clinging mud, and slowly fares
To church, or pub, or war with foreign powers;

But, as a ship, or migrant bird, or deer
Moves in a limited orbit, driving back

[1] Eloff Street: one of the main streets of Johannesburg. The city itself
is built on an exceptionally dull rectangular grid.

On pre-determined courses, so with man;
His many-branching lungs are roots in air;
His eyes, mind, lips, have roots; and he is drawn
By vital tissues, dying if they crack.

South African

The walls jabber,
They whisper, chatter, argue,
Then jabber.
This is eight thousand feet down,
Two thousand below sea-level;
It's the pressure that makes them jabber—
As it does men sometimes,
Shriek, and then jabber, jabber.

The wall is low here,
The passage full of the noise of machinery,
Hundreds of mine-boys, iron-wheeled trolleys,
The sudden impact of blasting;

And then this casual readjustment
Of millions of tons of rock
With a tearing as of steel plates, a gun-report
Followed by this lunatic,
Straining, complaining jabber.

'You can tell by the note when they're going to burst,
Rocketing inwards;
This is still the warning jabber!'

A prick in the earth's crust,
Two of the four thousand miles to earth's centre;
But the piled plateau of the Highveld,

The Drakensberg mountains,
The South Atlantic and Indian oceans
Press on me as the walls
Jabber, jabber.

.   .   .   .   .

His eyes are rooted in these accidents
Of soil, and crops, and buildings: mealie-fields—
Massed shafts and blades of assegai; cowhide shields—
Split cobs with grain-row markings; vast extents

Of plumes wind-tossed by Zulu discontents;
This endless, undulating khaki veld,
Where upon sun-dried earth the ants have built
Their kraals of domed and hutlike tenements.

Now Europeans, the last invaders, bring
Their even undulations in square roofs
Of corrugated iron, and hear the ring
Of hailstones on them—the stampeding hoofs
Of cattle, curved horns crowding; dour as ants
Pile up square dumps beside their tribal haunts.

R. N. CURREY

From *Ultimate Exile*

How lovely are the waters of Babylon
Removed three thousand years, three thousand miles;
The weeping willows green in the dusty plain,
And, in the dusk, to the cricket's insistent buzz,

The sound of harps and weeping, without pain
For us, at this great distance, after this time . . .

How wonderful, to sit in a cinema
And have your war brought to you; El Alamein,
A barrage like a black Niagara of sand,
A creeping giant holding by the hand
Pygmies who fall—and rise to run again:
The lurch and slither of a reptile band
Of belly-dragging tanks; strange sarabande
Of Engineers with long divining-wand
Moving ahead of the army and smelling out
Like devil-dancers the mines and boobies hidden
Under the wheel-cracked crust and crest of the sand;
The long untidy columns of famine-ridden
Scorched prisoners; the charred trunk and clenched hand
Of a dead enemy; the urgent shout
Of a sergeant to a devil-choir of guns;
All the excitement, all the thrill
Of modern warfare, the chase and the kill—
And the triumph! To watch with pleasantly-scalded eye
The spit-and-polish sporrans swinging by
Skirling *Cock o' the North* for victory—
And all for two shillings; sit in your seat
And never feel the brazen heat of the sun,
And the daze, and the beat, and the stun
Of the guns as they fire; the oven-heat
(Under the riveting hammer of the sun)
Of tanks rank with the stink of oil;
The smell of roasted flesh, that sweet sick smell;
The sick plague of flies spawned by the sun;
Sand like hot embers in the eye, in the groin.
The blind whirlpool of sand obscuring the sun;

79

The long hot monotonies, preoccupied
With sand in the limber, sand in the chamber,
Sand in the brakes, in the gears, in your hair;
The men that bear the burden and heat of the day
Have these thrown in and nothing extra to pay:
But the delicate edge between triumph and defeat
And the personal danger of death don't go with the seat—
Nor yet the occasional coolness after heat
And the occasional clear, bare
Unbelievable austerity of desert air,
Jewelling edges of sand, while mountains as far
As fifty miles away stand suddenly near
And pink as rose-petals in water,
O water—O the sheer
Cool of a pool leaf-hidden from the sun:
How lovely are the waters, the waters of Babylon.

R. N. CURREY

Marshal Lyautey[1]

My roads stretch out
Into the tamed interior;
My body lies
Beneath a Muslim dome in Christian soil.

My roads are rivers of trade,
My ports are open;
My soldiers rule by flags instead of blood,
Holding the ring for warlike tribesmen.

[1] Colonial administrator of genius, sometimes called the Rhodes of French North Africa.

My snow-fed rivers
No longer race to the sea, but stroll abroad
Beneath white birds
Among new farms and forests.

In the green corner of a civil service garden
Where Arabs scythe the grass,
I feel the miner's pick, the controlled explosion,
The engineer's step on the new barrage.

My feudal, feudal world should be quite perfect;
My sergeants and my Berbers know their places;
My Caids administer justice, but new nomads
Disfigure the land with shanty-town disgraces.

I tried to make a marriage of convenience
Between the Cross and the Crescent;
But the voice of Marx, professional seducer,
Corrupts the veiled, platonic bride.

My still hand still protects
The mosque, the ruined medersa,
The intricate craftsman and the singing fountain,
The flawless stupid face behind the veil.

R. N. CURREY

Morocco

Seven invasions, seven dynasties,
Seven cruel and splendid histories;
Seven dictators, seven capitals,
With tended minarets and crumbling walls;

The Romans, like the French, came to make roads;
The Carthaginians came for trade and war;
What brought the Berbers is a mystery
As strange as their occasional blond hair.

Islam that brought the Arabs baffles us,
Being infidels with no beliefs at all;
Their motives, like their mosques, are closed to us;
And each new dynasty that built a wall

Shared with this faith a common restlessness
That raised up gross Meknes and dappled Fez,
Gray Moulay Idriss, ochre Marrakech,
And Rabat ruling from white offices;

And now the restlessness that brought them here
Diverts the Gulf Stream Drift of history,
To throw back on the shores of Africa
A New World's Voyages of Discovery.

R. N. CURREY

Landscape

Many have planted
Individual kindnesses
But stones have stunted
Their tender growth;

Roots are twisted
By suspicion,
Humiliation
Eats the shoots.

In this hard land
In an hour
The sun can burn up
Root and flower

As men are burned, but ash
Of petal and skull
Fails to enrich
The bitter soil.

R. N. CURREY

Song

There is no joy in water apart from the sun,
There is no beauty not emphasized by death,
No meaning in home if exile were unknown;
A man who lives in a thermostat lives beneath
A bell of glass alone with the smell of death.

There is no beauty like that seen from a cliff;
The beauty of women comes and goes with a breath;
A man must offer the beauty of his wife
In sacrifice to give his children breath—
The children will walk on their folded hands of death.

Nothing in life is near and nothing far
Apart from love; a man can live beneath
His roof more lonely than an outer star;
And know a woman's beauty, a flower's breath
Walking alone in the valley of the shadow of death.

R. N. CURREY

Durban Revisited

After these weeks at sea, my native land:
I stand and stare at the remembered Bluff;
Enough that long green skyline for a boy,
The joy of those high breakers, their huge roar
Upon the shore, the lift-in of the tide.

A forefather in eighteen-forty-eight
In state landed his family here; his blood
Has flowed up almost every fertile valley;
But many of his sons, through circumstance,
Lost his intense and civilized tolerance.

By chance we ride at anchor in the Bay
A day or two, and may not go ashore;
Once more between me and this lovely land
There stands a barrier; it used to be
My childhood, now it's my maturity.

R. N. CURREY

In Memoriam: Roy Campbell

He grew where waves ride nine feet high
Like Zulu impis up the beach
Crested with sound, and every boy
Must watch for the whites-of-eyes of each.

84

Long rollers, horned like bulls, would gore
Into the whinnying groins of sand,
And every boy, a matador,
Must hold his courage out, and stand.

He learned to watch the rush and lunge,
And feel his feet, and wait until
The instant came for him to plunge
Into the envy poised to kill;

To plunge, and come through to a world
Of triumph on the other side,
Where he is lifted up and whirled
Down the long combers of his pride.

N. H. BRETTELL

From *Wind and an Eagle Owl*

We rode out with the pealing day before us,
Down plains all wind and woods in trouble,
With the first tooth of winter in the air:
All the world's sullen doors blew open for us—
Crippled and craven, the plovers scattered crying
On the shouldering air, peevish, lamentable:
And in a fence, the great bird trapped and dying
With splintered scapulars spreadeagled there—
You luckless fellow of our night of wind,
Who through the breathing solitudes had hunted,
And blindly struck like us, but not with us had sinned,
Now broken on the barbs that we had blunted.

I tie my timid filly up
To get a stick to kill you with;
With pity brimming like a cup,
I come your murderer in disguise:
Your great beak gaped in savage grin,
Your great stare narrowed to a frith
Of gleaming horror and surprise,
And oh the wells of hatred in
Your wildwood eyes, your wildwood eyes.

N. H. BRETTELL

Elephant

Slowly the great head turned,
And the late sunlight slept on massive flanks
Like the still slabs of riven krants,[1]
Immovable, and nonchalantly bearing
The burden of the old enormous lies,
The load of legendary centuries,
The mighty turtle and the seas of milk
On which the old World swam;
And slowly folded back the fluted ears
Like pterodactyl's wings drooping to roost.

Slowly the great limbs moved:
The monstrous pistons in the wrinkled sheath,
Unflurried and unhesitating, lift
The huge façade across the afternoon:
Like a great engine, headed north,

[1] Krantz: cliff.

With the deliberation of the six-foot wheels
Slides from the vaulted terminus
Down miles of metals through a continent.
Behemoth, baron, lord,
—In trigger-fingered world, one creature left unscathed;
Away from us, over the burnt earth, under the forest branches,
Casually stripping the green crown from a tree,
Going oblivious, the invulnerable beast.

N. H. BRETTELL

Giraffes

Framed in the sedan windows, the tall triangular faces
Watched us with distant interest above the green
Fringed parasols of the immense acacias
That scattered their point-devise in shady places,
      And the heat shimmer lay between.

Out-focused through lorgnette or quizzing-glass,
Neck inter-crossing neck, glance backward from between
Serpentine vertebrae, harmless and mild as doves,
With velvet hornlets topped, leisured they pass,
      Innocent, epicene:

Till with their five attenuated limbs,
With gestures of a slowly geared machine,
They pick up distance on an enormous hand,
Outpacing my fantastic synonyms:
      The sedan windows quivered in between.

Slowly the sedans pass:
With lamplight and link-light bobbing on the strings
Of smooth blond faces down the boulevards,
And paint and patch behind the discreet glass
Attend the whispered tryst, the slow pavane, the cards,
The coy queens and complacent kings,
All the brocaded faded go-betweens,
And centuries remote beyond the sedan windows.

You grave quaint harlequins, to deceive us
With the gay curves of kirtle and crinoline
In a grey wilderness. Reluctantly leave us,
While the incessant grasshoppers scissor away the minutes;
                    O lost arcadian scene,

O happy groves: centaur or unicorn prances
Across the hourless wastes that lie between
Our watchful present and the wistful bygones,
When the bland century and our budding fancies
                    Were both eighteen.

N. H. BRETTELL

Outside Kimberley

So, sick at heart, we watched the piccanins,
The sparrows bickering round our waiting train,
With thin capering shanks and cocked cunning eye
Waiting the casual scraps of charity,
The broken biscuit, half-smoked cigarette,
As restless minnows worry around the bait,

Glint of white eyeball, hungry flurry of fins:
What urchin avarice, goblin and devilish,
Each for himself, soul-less as bird or fish—
And, pricking at our scalp, the vague alarms,
Surprising inner pink of apish palms
And tongue and gaping gums.

There were the infamous slums,
The sprawling leprous lichens,
Battered tin roofs and corrugated shacks:
The leering door where scrap of sack discloses
The fetid doss-rooms and the stinking kitchens,
The heavy dust that lolled upon the air,
And the demented children screeching there,
While our defeated hearts stood reaching there:
Indignant of such things behind our backs,
Behind our backs, under our delicate noses,
Beneath the evening's avenues of bronze.

The train moved us on, we happy holiday ones,
Over the empty desecrated plain
Which the kind hour touched with pastel finger
Framing in level lines of mauve and grey
The path of one lost antelope—
Yes, with a gentle lifting of the heart, we saw him,
One solitary springbok, picking his way
With slow fastidious steps amid the dusty tufts:
Lovely lonely cousin,
Lonely survivor of the lovely herd
Who once in white and chestnut multitude
In centuries and thousands fed and frolicked
And kicked the dust from off a million acres:
Now going sad and elegant, like us, doomed family.

N. H. BRETTELL

Cataclysm

('Othello' at Stratford)

Beneath the fourteen pointed arches
The cool draught stirs the gillieflowers;
The petals on the dust-enmarbled water
Pollen and gold of many summer hours
Float where the assembled swans
Accept the casual flattery and the crumbs.
The idle punt and pinnace loiter down
Lipping the tidy lawns; now and again there comes
Through faltering willows and slow-ripening fruit,
Through avenues of slow-maturing years,
Where the sleek green Triton's shoulder of the chute
Breaks to the tumble of foam,
The round-the-corner rumour of the weirs.

It's half-past one. The pleasant playday crowd
Waits on the green and lets the petals slide.
It's half-past one: the Moor, somewhere inside,
Daubs on the dun complexion of his shame.
Soon the cold trumpets will proclaim aloud
The pomp and circumstance: the violins
Insinuate the insult and the blame,
The half-remembered interrupted song
That lifts and falters like a very willow leaf.
And ever from our seated helplessness,
The sidelong hint, the word, the handkerchief,
Like straws whirl on the inevitable flow—
Leaving us all just Roderigo.

Aloof as swan or water hyacinth,
The smooth stream glides beneath the solid stone,
Voissoir and pier and plinth—
The reassurance of the centuries
We lean our wistful wishes on
To shun the vertigo of the swirling years.
The plot swings steadily down towards the weirs:
How further must we drift, before
The testy senators tumble us into war?

ADÈLE NAUDÉ

The Oracle of Delphi

And after all, it's there for the listening—
Not in the vapours or the laurel spray
For Pythia's long dead or fled, her spring
Of wisdom stilled by the dusty overlay

Of time. No, not in these, not in the spoken
Word, but asleep in the stone and in the field.
Deep is the oracle, deeper than token
Pillar and broken metope, sealed

In the very heart of Delphi. There, when Apollo
Rides down the sky and evening levels the edge
Of day bevelled by his radiance, follow
The Sacred Way, then climbing high to a ledge,

Rest beyond temple, theatre and time. So still
Here, where the surf of the first spring daisies breaking
Round your feet recedes from the ancient hill
As petals close, and the olive grove, snaking

To the sea, sloughs its silver in
The darkening ravine; here there is peace,
Only a far and lonely goat bell's thin
Small note and the froth of pink wild almond trees.

Only yourself now, shriven and purified
As though in the sacred spring of Castalia,
Cleansed in the silence of the mountainside,
The quiet welling of Parnassian air.

Here you will find the gods in your harmony
With Delphic stone and earth. Slowly you rise,
For in the presence of antiquity
The oracles emerge, deep solemn and wise.

ADÈLE NAUDÉ

Memling's Virgin with Apple

She is a person here in her own right.
This one forgets when the Child, the three wise men,
holy angels and shepherds share the light
with her. So often she's but part of the composition,
part of the scene.

But here she's the centrepiece.

There's a Child, it's true, reaching a hand
for a glossy apple and rich embroideries
on His cushion. There's a cameo of a distant land.
But the landscape's far away, the trees
fading from the picture, the towers of the town
withdrawing themselves. The Child one hardly sees
although He is near. It is the blue of her gown
with the jewels, twin rivers of hair
held with a pearl-starred coronet, the glow
of the red cloak, the flowing hands. All is there
of purity in the lowered lids, the wide brow.

But there's a detachment and a strange withdrawal,
an aloneness in her serenity
taking her far away from us. It's unusual,
for mothers holding their children are not easily
disentangled. But she was different, I know.
There was no one quite like her. That's why,
Perhaps, the painter depicted her so—
a mother, but aloof, made lonely by the high
rôle she was playing. Special people would be
like that—kings and queens and very great
artists. Perhaps in this moment she,
for the first time, realizes her state
of separation. She was engaged before
with His hourly needs and the unfolding wonder
of motherhood. But here He is wanting more,
for He's older, wanting the shining object beyond her.
From this moment in the picture, onwards, her road
will be skirting the market-places, the cheering,
gossipy exchanges where a load
of strangeness might be lightened in the sharing.

From now onwards her state will be a lonely one
all through her life and when the chapter ends
in darkness, she'll stand with the other Marys, alone
and weeping in a wilderness of friends.

MARGARET ALLONBY

A Book for Christmas

From the North the populated breeze
Brings alive the flying messages.
Like leaves, red feet relinquish bonny trees.
In time for Christmas they have booked their passages,
Over Congo, across the red zone of heat.
The secret wind they know, in the southern hills,
Twists about them, curves their course. Their feet
Clasp last year's rest. How long, how long
The long month's cry, until our hearts are stirred
By thrilling news, the birds! We belong
Who, in these latitudes, with no word,
No confraternity, no song, cup ear
To catch the angel sounds, now near and here.

MARGARET ALLONBY

From *Lustration of the Winter Tree*

In this savage place the sun stands still,
Like Joshua's sun. Time does not condemn,
Does not approve. Time with all the shades
Of the superfluous is lost: all but
Time's question, time's threat and consequence,
Time's fear, fear brilliant. A voice, a mirage—
Flaming word like 'pentecost', 'prepare',
Accosts the mind that pauses here; a tongue.
Time asks: in the remnant of a fear turned hope,
Or hope turned fear, in the problem of the frontier,
It is a tongue like flame, a two-edged sword
Pressing its menace upon the inhabitant
In the logged and dying will. Time asks.

MARGARET ALLONBY

O Theophilus

(*To our helpers*)
He trembled for us
In our dark ages.
The minutes marched correct,
Eyes glass, towards the end.
Their drill, at last, was perfect.
Knowledge knew what to expect.

In the square, standing alone
Among the crowd, logic could calculate
Nothing but our chronic pain:
Saw us raise our arms,
Heard us lift our voices up
In declaration of despair

And indignation.
Beneath the Town Hall clock
We stated the reverberation
Of sjamboks, reiteration of Treks
To Pass Offices[1] where we affirmed
Negation, confirming our share,

Our choice of cruelty and hate.
We acknowledged devil-law, and our lot.
We recognized our disability.
We said to God, 'You made me black,'
Or, 'Why did my Dad leave Cumberland?'
We stood beneath the clock.

He climbed the face
Of the mighty dial of human crime:
He overcame its mighty power.
He grasped in time
With his bare hands the sabre edge
And took the strain.

Through the flaring smithy-cave
His current thrilled paralysis
In hell. The world he overcame
And made the clock-work feel.
Clutching the arrow-head of pain
The steeple-jack kept back the chime

[1] African males are obliged by law to carry passes.

Of doom and fixed it in his heart,
Held back the bells, for love of us,
To ring out the resurrection
Of the beauty of the universe,
Its meaning, beginning, now, forever,
Then. He trembles for us men.

In our Place of Discord, at the Pass Office,
In the suburban bioscope, in the Location,[1]
He speaks through our Theophilus
And keeps us in his promise
And blesses even us with his forever Yes.

MARGARET ALLONBY

For Sheila

Shingle, sand, sea, shells, the tracks
Of twin feet setting sole to sand.
The passive shore receives the air,
Persistent force devours the land.

Smoke is taken by lungs and air.
The sand sticks to the hand.
The piccanins take root and stare:
Missus in trousers from the Rand.

Voices under the sea are muted.
The puppies run away like the brook.
The sign creaks Trespassers Will Be Prosecuted.
Murder of My Uncle is the name of my book.

[1] Location: residential area for people of colour.

The voices, bold in the seventh wave,
Ask, 'If All wrong, All same wrong, So-&-So. So?'
The sea's for this; Wave rhymes with Grave.
The hurrying stream says, 'No no no . . .'

Should missus take the plunge and learn
The answer to the question-mark?
The sign creaks, the children look, the pages turn,
The dogs begin to bark.

'To obey what's better than ourselves,'
Wild Herman Melville said,
'We've got to disobey ourselves',
Not skulk beneath the ocean bed.

MARGARET ALLONBY

Eurydice

The dream has spilled its genial plenitude
Upon the dry Namaqua of the day.
Joy teemed. Allowed to be, I heard the speech
And watched the dance, the gracious looks, the talking
Hands of that so amiable throng,

And walked with them in pastures green.
Remembrance withers in the nothing-cave:
None would I invite to share the tenancy
And meet the shadows on the wall.
The orphic pull has gone.

What could guests hear? Rabid stuttering
Of oft-repeated syllables, drums of fear:
See zany witchmen jerk or coil or stamp,
Hyaenas, snakes, wildebeeste, scorpions
Deride, hiss, stampede, sting.

Mad saliva drips hydroptic to the dust-
To-dusty ground. Silvered on the funguses,
Mucous scales of sheer despair take reptile
Shape and breathe the musty, fetid air
That has been breathed before.

Aimless in filtered, sickly gloom, alone,
Separated, made blind and lank like leaf
Lacking chlorophyll, the inhabitant
Of a nowhere threads the minutes on a string
And wears a torque of tusks.

Subvocally I gibe at thought of sound
Of lute or look of light and if I heard
A human voice ring out 'Eurydice!',
As in a horror-dream, would not my tongue
Be dumb? My own 'Too late!'

Long since I heard re-echoed by the lost.
The war that once was all my passion
Vanished in that work. Across wild waves
Sometimes a summons shrieks its pain.
Denunciation shuts my ears.

But, then, that other way I saw: not a dream!—
And should there shimmer a lance of light
And should there show a western path and I

Be beckoned once again, as then, my eyes
Perceive that blazed and harrowed avenue
Made then, by an ineffable descent,
Could I elect to totter forth
And yet not take the cave with me?

MARGARET ALLONBY

Reflection

Beneath the brown, lustrous haze,
A lit tulle stretched across the brackish spruit,[1]
The tree contorts and, innocent,
More antique than Eve's considering,
    Moves Babylonian arms.

The brown look glazes the intricate design.
The deep roots stir, the sun is hypnotized
And the wind drops; the long hair stirs
In the brown summer, felicity evolves
    A nautch of rippled limbs.

From inmost bole as if from lungs
Must the music to evoke such strange chromatic dances
Come Siam to western ears but subtler
Untranslatably through the finger-tips, till dying
    Ebb the cadent rhythms.

Above, the watcher in the suspense
Of symphony lies along the pulmonary willow-bough;

[1] Spruit: small stream.

Hands sleep along the branch: but the heart
Beats foreign. The breath, drawn down, revives
    The exhausted enthusiasm.

The corroboree begins again. She feeds on me,
The watcher feels, who fights: my X-ray eyes meet hers
In the sunflash on the sudden edge of ripple,
The optic pinnacle of water hard as glass,
    Fixed in the moment's speculum:

My down-fall hers; her fight, my victory,
In tree-bound fixity of roots that seek release. Though fast
In the past, the past shall move wherein
I lapse to labefaction's limit; glimpse,
    Only then, the theorem:—

The being is the being, miraculous; the river flows
In tree, tree in river, earth's innocence
In us. A freedom is in this. God
Is not maleness or malice aforethought,
    Is far above the hers and hims.

God is not trees—a tree supported Him. A brown blaze
—Aware experience is not innocence—
Reveals, in chanciness of myth,
Earth's maiden excellence in darkling dance,
    Simpler than psalms.

Image of image, the trees concur to be,
One real, one pictured, upon the soundless eye;
Unlike and like, through thought's medium, blaze
A world of envisaged forms, and on the foreign heart jot down
    A symbiosis of aims.

From *The Hours of the Planets*

Now English eyes the cancerous sun behold!
Bright over blackened Africa, Sahara
Futurity and all paluster lakes of sewage,
Utter blackness, uttering thundercloud
On native waste and villages of hut
Far as I can see
Earth's declivity is infinite
Falling away, fading in infinite forms
Horizon added to horizon.
Man stands black within the pause of thought
Shadowless perpendicular under beam
In deaf-mute equatorial solitude
When Fulmen falls, resounds among remaining mountains.

CHARLES MADGE

Delusions VIII

Placed in a country on a desert verging
But under southern skies, richer in stars,
I spent my solitary years observing
Their forms, more bright and numerous than ours.

They date from childhood, and the first dissection,
The bleached skull and the spiny xerophyte,
Those tastes, which taking gradual direction
With more mature experience unite.

My voyage in the ocean, where the lead
Was dropped into an unknown gulf profound
Explained some features of the secret bed:
In those domains I was the first to sound.

CHARLES MADGE

From *Poem by Stages*

I

To us, goddess, who are in barbary
Looking across unfortunate waters, hearing
All round those wordless voices of machines,
To us be kind, be good to us, your children,
Lead us across the wilderness, protect us
From tricks of time, exorcize for us
Moping demons, and cast for us
A fair horoscope when we set out

For we intend, goddess, to make a journey
By land and sea, and we can see no end
In our life nor in any life we know
Of children, or children's children undescried
And unconceived. And so please grant us grace
To give life

And to have life, through you, in words and forms
That will enact by generation,
By genital and scriptural tradition,
The story of our going.

The adventures of my separate bark
Were also not finished at Dragomestri.
To be brief, we had bad weather almost always.
We were twice upon the rocks.
My health is now better and I ride again.
We travelled due south along the coast,
Over a hard, stoneless, alluvial plain,
Here dry, there muddy (where the tide reaches)
Across boggy creeks, broad water-courses
And warty flats of black mould powdered
Bristling with salsolaceous vegetation.
Continued travelling through the wilderness
And the distant ridges of the hills
Seemed to waver in the ascending vapour
And fluctuate like the unsettled sea:
In vain, nothing appeared all round
But underwood and hillocks of white sand.
My thirst by this time insufferable,
I chewed the leaves of different shrubs,
The same dismal uniformity.
After a short but ineffectual struggle,
Here then (thought I) terminate all my hopes
Of being useful in my day and generation.

24

First, erected ironworks in a spiry hollow
Amazingly like England, and having crossed
The desert of table manners, invented coffee
In two or three generations (compare
The longevity of painted rock faces).
Oddly: it was grandfather stumbled over

The oldest skull of all, digging a ha-ha!
In spite of these finds, lived leisurely
Hiving civilizations imperceptibly
Making, melting male female colossal
Effigies in whose shadows the world changed
And the topsoil incorporated
The blazon of their summers, rags, buttons
An aunt, an unrepeatable infant
The substance, best and worst, crumbled by fingers
Of moiling creators in gardens.
Frequently self-expelled by longitude and
Latitude (lions usual at the bus stop)
Attacked internally by the native problem
(Who sweat poison) adopted compromise positions
All over the globe, and made one world
Out of their own crass intransigence.

31

The flesh is sad but there are books unread.
Time always was too short in that respect.
But when at night the children are in bed
The light is kind on the unwritten sheets
And voyages I may not undertake. Oh steamer
Lost in lamp's shadow, other alchemists,
Waiting release at their own funerals
In a myrrh of parting, in a tangent smoke
Diffuse, elsewhere, on a grey evening.
There are families of china, families of plants
And isolated groupings in the sand
And a receding daylight, vast and dim
With hardly a foothold for a fly
On the transparent cross-beams up aloft.

32

Among all the myths and masks and make-believes
Is the solid marvel in the antique bed,
A decent idol. Long washed in the tides
Of the spring estuary, the salted stone
Is big and smooth. Abundant are the waters.
I can rest here, the waves lapping beside.
And all dead things all corpses and corruptions
Are cleaned into a flotsam of hard shapes,
Are in reversion are made whole again.

F. T. PRINCE

The Babiaantje

Hither, where tangled thickets of the acacia
Wreathed with a golden powder, sigh
And when the boughs grow dark, the hoopoe
Doubles his bell-like cry,
Spreading his bright striped wings and brown crest
Under a softening spring sky,—
I have returned because I cannot rest,
And would not die.

Here it was as a boy that, I remember,
I wandered ceaselessly, and knew
Sweetness of spring was in the bird's cry,
And in the hidden dew
The unbelievably keen perfume
Of the Babiaantje, a pale blue
Wild hyacinth that between narrow grey leaves
On the ground grew.

The flower will be breathing there now, should I wish
To search the grass beneath those trees,
And having found it, should go down
To snuff it, on my knees.
But now, although the crested hoopoe
Calls like a bell, how barren these
Rough ways and dusty woodlands look to one
Who has lost youth's peace!

F. T. PRINCE

In a Province

Because of the memory of one we held dear
Call to mind where she lived and the ruins there
Among the silken shrubs. I have dismounted where
Her children played and watch the pale sky grow clear.

And as for me, standing between the silken shrub and the
        broom
And tasting the breath of the blue sage, I must stay
Though my friends are setting out with the first of the day
And they murmur to me, 'Do not linger in that gloom,
Remember that tears make whole the heart.' But I say
'Is there nowhere I may rest among the shells
Of the ruins and the droppings of white gazelles?
However brief my hours are, I would delay.'

The tears that fall from my eyes have wet my hands
Holding the reins of my horse. How many hours
Were sweet to me because of women! These showers
Bring to my mind that day among pale sands,

107

Call to mind how one came with me unwillingly
On an evening warm as another country's noons
And all seemed of long ago among those dunes
And under a clear sky, under a clear green sky.

F. T. PRINCE

False Bay

She I love leaves me and I leave my friends
In the dusky capital where I spent two years
In the cultivation of divinity.
Sitting beside my window above the sea
In this unvisited land I feel once more
How little ingenious I am. The winter ends,
The seaward slopes are covered to the shore
With a press of lilies that have silver ears.
And although I am perplexed and sad I say
'Now indulge in no dateless lamentations;
Watch only across the water the lapsed nations
And the fisherman twitch a boat across the bay.'

F. T. PRINCE

Chaka

I. The King Watches at Night
The air cool and soft,
The darkness early about this sorrow, I
Am alone awake, I am alone

To watch the trembling of so many tears
Above my hard and empty lands. The plain
Mutilated and scarified, with dust and ashes on a black face
Looks brittle as a moth's wing. Shall I weep?

The cattle had been gathered in the village, the leader
Bellowed on two dull notes, when
Passing a poor woman's hut I sniffed her hearth of curds and
    embers
At dusk under the grey smoke of a dung-fire
I heard her call her babes to supper and saw
The too-big-bellied urchins
Come clustering to the porridge-pot. And I thought
'You have done well for yourself,
But it is not very long
Since you would run weeping home because of the thunder
When the storm threw the old trees on their chins.'

Often night lets down darknesses upon me
And every kind of doubt to weigh upon me. Then
I have said to him, as he thrust out his breast,
As he leapt forward like a pitch-black bullock,
As he buttocked with his buttocks
I have said, 'Night
Are you not coming to an end because of dawn?'
And he murmurs back, the night,
'You go too far, you have gone far enough.'

I have wandered out in the thin tang of white stars
While my friends were asleep below the hills.
Depending only on rumours of my starry meals
It was not for them to know how far my gaze was set.

II. He Compares Old Customs with Those of His Kingdom

There would come up many idle men to sit with the strangers
And sit down at our side. How they puffed off their words!
They would ask us what ancestry we were of;
We would tell them that and tell them
How for our ancestors we set apart
A bit of a broken pot or a forked stick
It might be, in the hut, or a little shrine
As who should say, a set of stones
Carefully selected, with a tree growing up in the middle:
Or how there might be a special sacred tree or grove of trees
Or finally there might be a true tomb
Used as a temple.

The variations might be innumerable
But there would be always remembrance,
It would be always as we said
Although the manner of our remembrance varied.
There might be libations of beer,
There might be gifts on those altars
Of all that men use for food;
There might be prayers and appeals from those in trouble.

And they replied and they said
'We think well of these men
Who it seems will be far off on some high place
Perhaps, by the day dawning.'
And they made us sit down again
To hear again how we reverenced the dead
And filled up our pipes with sweet herbs
Although they had not half enough for themselves.

But now the old men and the infirm have been well killed.
Now there are spies who crawl back from the south
Bearing on cheeks and shanks the sores
Of a new sickness. They will be burned. And there are captains
Who have returned from failure, to be hanged.
And my singing messengers have taxed the coast,
My soldiers weep with hurry at my commands.
They go out to slay, they return at night weary of slaughter,
They advance and attack and outflank and flee all at once.
And on the most desirable of my hills
In the sweetest of fastnesses I speak well of them.

And I have divided the captives, allotted them ranks,
From time to time thus I established
Twenty-five regiments.
Some wear a headdress of otter-skin, others of leopard-skin,
The wing-feathers of the eagle or the ostrich
Are commonly added to these
But the red wing-feathers of the green lory
Are worn only by royal grant.
And I have given them names,
Called my regiments Decoys,
Slashers, Gluttons or else Bees
Ambushes, Mountains, the Blue Haze.
So we had too a name in the world
And war was our host in these places (there was blood in
    the dregs of the cup).

And so with white or black ox-tails, kilts of leopard-skin
And the broad shields of stretched cow-hide
White or brown with a crimson or with a black spot,
They went out. So my state
Was fanned by a frond of fern and in the red shadow

Of cloud-like trees I was repaid.
Among gossip of moist leaves, tongues of an upstart court
To my gaudy establishment as general
Many emissaries, bitter, brought the crane's feather
And offered many tokens to placate, including
Sea-shells and a quantity of melons.

III. *How Festivals were Celebrated*

The eyelid severed from its terrible schemes
Is reproached by a leafage of numberless small flames.
Tenderness is peculiarly active
In the first days of spring weather.
The province is all astir with fronds and buds
And when one walks out in the meadows a sweet steam
Floats up beneath one's foot. A scarlet tree
Lit by the late wet season to her tips
Sways and offers to the man who sways a scarlet crown
And shakily a man's mind
Controls its longing to be spilt,
A couple of dew-drops lying
In the hollow of a leaf.
So a man may be slain for his eminence in dancing
When the plain is alive with hair-like flowers!
At last there will be something to be said
That I have made my own.

I have brought fear to this people,
I have rendered them as rich and smooth as ox-blood.
But am I a bird of prey that I pursue
Only after the scent of a carcass? I might say
How with my lust I have refreshed the laws,
Giving out orders to hoe: and in the autumn
How some were allotted new wives.

How after my hunting they passed many hot days
Tossing the meat the one to the other
And laughing at the fat that hung in tassels.
The condemnation of the warriors at an end,
Those who might die with the chief I kissed on the breast and
dismissed.

And there were the high days of the mind, the days of high
feasting
There were the feast days when, bare as a bolt
I danced before the people: as, on a dumb waste of green
grasses
And lilies tangled like a sheep's wet back
When the dawn's light was snowy in the sky and under foot
Light bubbled up and trickled to my foot. And on an evening
Wreathed with fond hues when the red rock
Smoked with a soft flame it had sucked
And when the washed air with that flush
Was burdened, I might have cried I was puffed up
With gross and fanciful enjoyments. Holidays
When on the smooth floor of a public place
As if in the teeth of all things I would act
As thunder, commandeer an echoing tube
And a congratulatory drug. And there were days
When the young sky was like a lake, but softer,
And to my voice, to purify the army,
The rivers once down, to depart in the dust
Of a perfumed month, a month
Of pollen, we devised a long dance before bathing.

IV. He Bathes in the Morning
Wings rise, the shrubs flutter.
I have bathed in this solitary water

And by the pool beside the flowering thorn
I turn a question over in my hands.
And in the opinion of this palest empty dawn
When a couple of birds to mock are making apart a single song
Which of us can forgive himself? for all are,
The song says, guilty of all.

The odour of journeys mingles with despair.
If the branches of the sweet-thorn are all broken,
They have been broken for our sins. Yet everywhere
The sweet-thorn with an odour
Of honey pains the deep waste of this hour of penitence.
The male bird gives a whistle
And his companion caps it like a bell,
And there is only this, that we are worthy.

V. *The People Rest after Conquests*

Such were the gifts inflicted upon us who trembled
At their brilliance. And a sharp rain
Having poured, we stretch ourselves in the sun to heal.
The hills are like old men sitting in their blankets,
The wild things are gay. Buck jumps, hawk dives.
And at the tip of that peak, like a knot
Of white spittle in a brown pool, see, that cloud
Softly clinches peace. The deepest colour,
The most mysterious, that of our flesh tells
We have eaten luminous shadows. We smoke hemp
And the conversation of some swallows is both a keen burden
And sweeter than that of the dead. And the foot-hills grow
    rosy,
A leopard-skin is trodden beside the enraptured river
And stretched on the glossy backs of boulders. The woman is
    panting,

Her dugs hang forward as she leans; as for her daughter,
She is light and dreadful as a spear, she too leaves a gash.

We clap our hands together. What do you dance,
What do you dance? We ask. We clap hands. How
Is it one sings your king's name? We have dreamed
Of an adorable authority and the brooks
Sobbing absurdly in the bright morning, the brooks
Glitter. There is so often news,
Yet we listen for news of the Men of the Sun, and of the Mist,
We murmur against the Men of the Baboons and those of
    the Showers,
We learn of the Men of the Little Bluebuck, the Men of the
    Young Lions,
Of the Sons of the Dancers of Iron and of the Children
Of the Elephant. All these are ours
And we are the People of Heaven. Tell us no lies
On our noons made loud by abolished clans.

ROY FULLER

The Green Hills of Africa

The green, humped, wrinkled hills: with such a look
Of age (or is it youth?) as to erect the hair.
They crouch above the ports or on the plain,
Under the matchless skies; are like the offered
Shoulders of a girl you only half know.
What covers them so softly, vividly?
They break at the sea in a cliff, a mouth of red:
Upon the plain they are unapproachable,
So massive, furrowed, so dramatically lit.

115

Can you be much surprised at what the hills
Contain? The girls run up the slope,
Their oiled and shaven heads like caramels.
Behind them is the village, its corrugated
Iron and, like a wicked habit, the store.
The villagers cough, the sacking blows from the naked
Skin of a child, a white scum on his lips.
The youths come down in feathers from the summit.
And over them all a gigantic frescoed sky.

The murder done by infinitesimal doses,
The victim weaker and weaker but uncomplaining.
Soon they will only dance for money, they'll
Discover more and more things can be sold.
What gods did you expect to find here, with
What healing powers? What subtle ways of life?
No, there is nothing but the forms and colours,
And the emotion brought from a world already
Dying of what starts to infect the hills.

ROY FULLER

The Plains

The only blossoms of the plains are black
And rubbery, the spiked spheres of the thorn,
And stuffed with ants. It is before the rains:
The stream is parched to pools, occasional
And green, where tortoise flop; the birds are songless;
Towers of whirling dust glide past like ghosts.
But in the brilliant sun, against the sky,

The river course is vivid and the grass
Flaxen: the strong striped haunches of the zebra,
The white fawn black, like flags, of the gazelles,
Move as emotions or as kindly actions.
The world is nothing but a fairy tale
Where everything is beautiful and good.

At night the stars were faint, the plateau chill;
The great herds gathered, were invisible,
And coughed and made inarticulate noises
Of fear and yearning: sounds of their many hooves
Came thudding quietly. The headlights caught
Eyes and the pallid racing forms. I thought
Of nothing but the word *humanity*:
And I was there outside the square of warmth,
In darkness, in the crowds and padding, crying.
Suddenly the creamy shafts of light
Revealed the lion. Slowly it swung its great
Maned head, then—loose, suede, yellow—loped away.
O purposeful and unapproachable!
Then later his repugnant hangers-on:
A pair of squint hyenas limping past.
This awful ceremony of the doomed unknown
And innocent victim has its replicas
Embedded in our memories and in
Our history. The archetypal myths
Stirred in my mind.

            The next day over all
The sun was flooding and the sky rose tall.
Where rock had weathered through the soil I saw
A jackal running, barking, turning his head.
Four vultures sat upon the rock and pecked,

And when I neared them flew away on wings
Like hair. They left a purple scrap of skin.
Have I discovered all the plains can show me?
The animals gallop, spring, are beautiful,
And at the end of every day is night.

ROY FULLER

The Tribes

I think of the tribes: the women prized for fatness
Immovable, and by a sympathetic
    Magic sustaining the herds,
    On whose strange humps sit birds;

And those with long dung-stiffened capes of hair,
And those that ceremonially eat their dead;
    The ornamental gashes
    Festered and raised with ashes;

The captured and dishonoured king compelled
To straddle a vertical and sharpened stake,
    Until, his legs hauled at,
    The point burst from his throat;

And all the prohibitions and the cheapness
Of life so hardly got, where it is death
    Even to touch the palace
    And poison expresses malice.

Now in the white men's towns the tribes are gathered
Among the corrugated iron and
      The refuse bins where rats
      Dispute with them for scraps.

Truly, civilization is for them
The most elemental struggle for bread and love;
      For all the tabus have gone,
      It is man against man alone.

On waste plots and in the decrepit shanties
They begin to discover the individual,
      And, with the sense in time
      Of Adam, perpetrate crime.

The most horrible things you can imagine are
Happening in the towns and the most senseless:
      There are no kings or poison,
      Are laws but no more reason.

ROY FULLER

In Africa

Parabolas of grief, the hills are never
Hills and the plains,
Where through the torrid air the lions shiver,
No longer plains.

Just as the lives of lions now are made
Shabby with rifles,
This great geography shrinks into sad
And personal trifles.

For those who are in love and are exiled
Can never discover
How to be happy: looking upon the wild
They see for ever

The cultivated acre of their pain;
The clouds like dreams,
Involved, improbable; the endless plain
Precisely as it seems.

TERENCE HEYWOOD

Cactus

Follow the ribs of my thought, lines
rocketing into the shadows of the mind,
that vault where they converge upon
a coral-beaded cactus-boss.

Watch me walking down the street,
    young, sporting a fine cane
with cactus-top that scatters beams;
    or old, leaning on it (knob the same).

There is a door opening on the desert
(stark certainty of the earth's skeleton):
notice how my hands fondle
the dear visionary protuberance of its handle.

I fondle what has shown affection
    in the poignant intimacy of its needles:
they have sewn wounds and have injected
    a purpose, and I have known healing.

TERENCE HEYWOOD

Mantis

Square-stanced hind-legs; body rectangular;
colour a broad-bean green-brown;
forelegs rigidulous; a tapering neck;
two broad arms, peaked upwardly, angular;
head, eye glittering, a rotund speck:
such I discern as I lean down.

TERENCE HEYWOOD

A Flamingo's Egg

See how it is teed up on the nest, enabling
my fancy to whack it down the fairway of the future.
Hatched, growing its own wings, it soars
over the barren bunkers of commonsense
and the despicable water-hazards of apathy, until
dizzyingly winning it dips for the piscine hole.

Now I am standing them all a drink: they are all
bibbers at the bar of beauty, their ears sprouting
tentacles that suck me dry. The central figure
in this vicarious beauty-snatching, I stand aloof,
nonchalantly surveying the naïve, and enjoy my triumph.

TERENCE HEYWOOD

By an Ant-Heap

Within this termitary
is no dormitory.
    Sexless and blind,
the workers bustle
along the tunnels
    with soldier guides.

There is no frillery
in any gallery:
all is for use,—
thrown-up food,
carcases, excrement
(eaten for increment,
then used for building).
All is utility:
the fattened queen's
an egg-machine.

            The king alone,
                    small as a commoner
        beneath her corpulence,
        sits in indolence
                    and is forgotten.

        Yet it is he
        who gives the seed—
        who has been the father
        of more than half.

What does it matter?
    when they are old
        (the royal couple),
when the queen miscarries
    or eggs come slow,
            no one will trouble
to bring them food:
all is for use
and themselves are food.

TERENCE HEYWOOD

Grisaille

I have seen lace-makers in Madeira,
    young girls laughing as with fingers nimble
they lightly embroidered the shroud of their short-lived sight.
            Laugh, girls, laugh, for you may as well,
    you who forget that every thimble
        's a funeral bell.

I have seen gold-miners in Africa
    thousands of feet under, and have heard them
        singing
crude monotonous songs in Zulu and Sesuto.
            Sing, boys, sing while the heart is young,
    for the earth has phthisical echoes, bringing
        dust to the lung.

123

I have seen road-menders in Piccadilly,
muscular youths exchanging casual jokes
as the rattling shattering road-drill battered the blocks.
Jest, lads, jest till the dread year comes
when the drill, not you, shall crack the jokes,
splitting the ear-drums.

But wherever I have gone I have seen young
people
for whom the nodal present is an empty pit,
the past but a vast worm-casting, and the future
a blank.—It is these unfit for suffering
I rather
pity than those whom living has made fit.
Pity them, Father.

ANTHONY DELIUS

Chameleon

Ancient and leaden-lidded he treads
A branch's tight-rope balancing his double times
Unsteadily, a calculating creeper stirs
Something alive out of extinct tellurian dreams.

Age with blood as green as youth,
Gay as a pigmy sunset painted on a leaf,
A crouching abstract of the sky
And flower and earth, savage in arthritic grief.

Suffers the puppy's caress
Of a bounding wind, unsoftened and not yet undone,
Watching behind his painted walls
In a small darkness, spun on a broken axle of sun,

Juggles the two hemispheres
On the black ridge of our old dilemma, plies
His patient, palaeolithic anger
With a hissing tongue on a diet of present flies.

ANTHONY DELIUS

The Coming

Today I found lean winter's
footprint in the dust
between boerboom[1] and cactus
on a lost road's crust.

The bush rang with his coming
rumour hung like smoke
along the empty channel
where a dead man spoke.

And an old wheel went turning
reminiscing on its own
took a wavering journey
over sand and stone.

[1] Boerboom: a leguminous tree with a dark red flower.

The leafy brains of bluegums
seismographed a storm
and air was filled with eddies
of dissolving form.

On a grey field's border
five black women moved
with on their head elliptic
bundles of dry wood,

five soundless notes of music,
slow long-skirted tread
that bore away the summer
to a country of the dead.

ANTHONY DELIUS

The Gamblers

The Coloured long-shore fishermen unfurl
their nets beside the chilly and unrested sea,
and in their heads the little dawn-winds whirl
some scraps of gambling, drink and lechery.

Barefoot on withered kelp and broken shell,
they toss big baskets on the brittle turf,
then with a gambler's bitter patience still
slap down their wagering boat upon the surf.

Day flips a golden coin—but they mock it.
With calloused, careless hands they reach
deep down into the sea's capacious pocket
and pile their silver chips upon the beach.

ANTHONY DELIUS

The Explorer

Three days from the Luapula still
A tree points out his final star,
A root keeps cradled in its dreamless fist
A tea-tin of his vital dust—
We hide no deeper mineral
In the dark ores of Africa.

I cannot specify what kind
Of tree, if it gives sweet or bitter fruit
Above the heart of Livingstone;
But yet it shivers as the sun
Returns, and in the fumbling mind
Of earth a pulse knocks on the root;

Seeks distance speaking like the restless drums
And routes to map the reefs below,
Our sources of enslavement he
Marks in a dark geography,
Still in his pilot-cap he plumbs
Rivers we bleed but do not know.

Look, from those depths another tree
Rears to the vortex of a vulture's eye,
The sun lolls like a saviour's head
High over the riven watershed,
And lithe beasts of deliverance lie
Red-clawed on branches in the sky.

He stumbled through the ritual disgrace
Below, and lipless winds blew pale
With drifts of bone the plains he trod
Nor knew they rose from where our blood
With rumour of huge Falls would race
To Benin and to Passchendaele.

But easier in thought he stepped
A Christian presence in the caravan,
And paced the width of evil, drove
A lurching heart beside the slave,
Furnished an ear to darkness, kept
An eye awake in hell for man.

Now bird-wing whispers out his myth
Creaking above the supple flood
Or game trails such as branched his broken marches
When thirty fevers fell—still searches
The listening ear of silence with
His little sibilance of blood,

And tall remembering shadows hold
Him bent above the growing chart
Of savage and amazing truth,
The first to care in all their growth
And at one's foot his human mould
Laid by at last the whispering pen and heart.

ANTHONY DELIUS

The Pilgrims

Many a green-fezz pilgrim falters
As family shrieks a welcome home
and feels the world-weight in his body
lean down across the aerodrome,
and shadows long as Africa
behind him touch an ancient qualm
at some unknown companion left
sleeping in dust on the Red Sea's arm.

A faint muezzin mocks him still
from a far interior minaret,
'See, the great meteorite in black
and stays impenetrable yet.'
And through a second's split he stares
at what he went so far to find,
the sanctuary's inner veil
hangs at the back of every mind.

So many I have watched come down
the gangways to themselves, returning
hearts gay with a dozen labels,
the same attache-case of yearning;
the world worn simply from the shoulder,
hung in the ear a foreign splendour,
persona stamped with many postmarks
and here, at last, returned to sender.

Each journey is a pilgrimage
to cross ourselves on many a shore,
go through the cracked mirrors of mankind
to find someone we've met before—
yet to Mecca he insists we go
by charter plane or K.L.M.,
connect at Kano or Zanzibar
for Mecca or Jerusalem.

London, New York have holy ghosts,
Paris and Amsterdam give grace
to those who lose the sense of touch
and man in a familiar place
and, sailing, cause the rolling skies
to turn through many faint degrees
till teeming coasts and cities hang
a healing hem of tapestries.

Art, Holy Footprint, I embrace.
O Thames, O Ganges wash me clean
of fate. My time be fresh white sands
I cross to find what feet have been
along Aegean coasts to seek
the single centres of devotion—
but deserts lie within my hands,
my veins have bled an Indian Ocean.

And far across great bones the route,
a healing serpent, writhes to cure,
the world is round and every path
must bite on its own tail once more;
and down past Atlas distance roots

the rocks that hear and sand that sees,
reaches the black man's commonwealth
and childhood dreaming in a buzz of flies.

The countries pour their many rivers
into the hold-all, brochures, trade,
seven wonders and stranger customs—
but St. Peter's, the Ka'abah fade.
The passing of land-birds overhead
I heard near dawn on every sea,
the dogged sky reforms, and home
myself shouts welcome from the quay.

ANTHONY DELIUS

From *The Great Divide*

Canto II
III

The ocean, with a calm sardonic titter,
Eyes what five centuries of trade have swirled
In tidal marks of civilizing litter
About 'the fairest Cape in all the world',
And in its lazy humour is a subtle
Blend of the lisping sand and broken shell,
And sea-weed brushed where the red crayfish scuttle,
And the creaking of some long-lost caravel.
White bones in the green hammocks rock below
Where Indian and Atlantic mix their waters,
Careless that whites ashore should grow
Hot about who should wed their great-granddaughters

And pour out laws that lovers from the seas
Must match in skin the ladies on their knees.

VII

But stricken with the high cafard, the town
Lies under heat as if beneath a feather quilt
And every gasp's like breathing eiderdown.
Even the gnus upon the mountain wilt;
Down in a hundred business occupations
The mind goes blank, dictating voices mute,
And writers writing books on race relations
Pause, falter in their feverish pursuit.
The Cape Times columnist leans forward, nods,
Knocking askew his culinary bays,
A local artist drops off as he prods
To daub more colour on the Cape Malays.
Sleep claims a score of Christian committees
From plans to turn their Coloured neighbours out—
There's no more pleasant pastime in the cities
Than pushing groups of other folk about,
Or, clearing out from schools for little whites
The duskier infants, sorting sheep from goats,
Bravely risking that such human slights
May make rejected children cut their throats.

XI

The Ethnic Anthem

'Ethnasia will last a thousand years,
Our land is studded with its glories,
Its monuments are separate bars
And segregated lavatories.
'God has through us ordained it so!
Post Offices are split in two

And separate pillar boxes fix
That correspondence does not mix,
No one has ever managed better
To guard the spirit—and the letter.

'On ethnic trains and buses daily hurry
Divided hues to earn divided bread,
The races may not fornicate or marry;
They even lie apart when they are dead.

'God may award his just damnation
For mixed or unmixed fornication;
Down here we warn the citizen
With whom it is a crime to sin,
And no man takes, with our cognizance,
A liberty without a licence.

'Yea, in our law men stand or fall
By rule of thumb or finger-nail;
So sensitive's our Roman-Dutch[1]
It notes if lips protrude too much.

'We've split all difference so fine—
No wider than a hair or skin,—
To foil the trick of traits and needs
So shockingly the same in breeds—
For such success in our researches
We thank Thee, Lord, in separate churches.

'How wondrous is our work, our way,
And thine as well, Great Separator,

[1] Roman-Dutch Law.

133

Who separating night from day
Left us to sort the rest out later.'

Let's say, the Opposition knows the ring
And is, quite often, wily in debate,
They bob and weave and use the ropes to spring
The classic punches of the bantam-weight.
Even with rabbit-punches, jabs and buts
Somehow they still appear too orthodox,
While all the fans yell out for blood and guts
They seem to deal in dictionary knocks,
And, dodging, make their stand for 'Integration'—
Their one great truth—their wordiest evasion!
And always when they're fiercest in the pressure
Spirit wanes, ardour suddenly gives out,
Their towering rightness shins it through a fissure,
Their thunderous presence fizzles to a doubt.
They have an odd political disease
Like epilepsy at 'Integration's' sound,
Abruptly see eternal verities,
Then fall deranged and rigid to the ground.
They can't decide to love or lose the black,
And so, to solve the irritating fix,
To free themselves and yet not feel his lack,
They want him 'taken out of politics'.
A Neth has only got to ask them 'How?'
And they retire to caucus and a row.

Oh, Jack St James can always cut a dash;
Even without a horse, his gay whip teases,
But will he turn out dexterous or rash

When his delight amid the uproar rises?
A Peter Pan of party politics,
Came to it young, it's kept him young too long;
Now age looks in, still plays the same old tricks
Impulsively, and still can play them wrong.
But one more sad behind his mask regrets
Himself lost leader of the English section,
Those for whom the old red sun subduedly sets
And maps grow chill with shadows of rejection.
These million English are a vague communion
Indifferent to leadership or goal,
Their most accomplished children flee the Union,
Search other countries for their cause and soul,
And to the pioneer premise of their fathers
Add on no better moral, finer story,
Leave our crude glaring sun and savage weathers
To bask, reflect in other people's glory.

XXXIII

And round these men spread the sub-tropic latitudes
Where flatness, vacancy and wind are features
With old dry beds of liberal beatitudes,
The haunt of nervous, vegetarian creatures,
And ostriches who swell their throats and mock
A lion's booming to the world around
But, when their heads are slipped into a sock,
Suffer indignities without a sound.
And look, a row of pretty antelopes
Are like inverted tripods at the back,
Klipspringer[1] liberals on rocky slopes,
Tread moral ledges safe from an attack.
Leaders prefer old wildebeests or gnus

[1] Klipspringer: a small antelope, with habits somewhat like the chamois.

Or pole-cats who can raise a stink at will,
And curse the rich constituencies who choose
This lofty breed that nibbles principle.
However, they, though posed upon their niches
Climb down when called to toe the party line
And then climb back to dream of final ditches,
And crises when they really do resign.

CHARLES EGLINGTON

Cheetah

Indolent and kitten-eyed,
This is the bushveld's innocent—
The stealthy leopard parodied
With grinning, gangling pup-content.

Slouching through the tawny grass
Or loose-limbed lolling in the shade,
Purring for the sun to pass
And build a twilight barricade

Around the vast arena where,
In scattered herds, his grazing prey
Do not suspect in what wild fear
They'll join with him in fatal play;

Till hunger draws slack sinews tight
And vibrant as a hunter's bow:
Then, like a fleck of mottled light,
He slides across the still plateau.

A tremor rakes the herds: they scent
The pungent breeze of his advance;
Heads rear and jerk in vigilant
Compliance with the game of chance

In which, of thousands, only one
Is centred in the cheetah's eye;
They wheel and then stampede, for none
Knows which it is that has to die.

His stealth and swiftness fling a noose
And as his loping strides begin
To blur with speed, he ropes the loose
Buck on the red horizon in.

CHARLES EGLINGTON

The Vanquished

With treble vivas and limp hedgerow flags
The children welcome us: again we meet
The fearful sons and daughters of defeat.
And through the town our dull compassion drags
The scarecrow of our greeting.
                                    Brown-eyed brat,
Your dusty face and sapless, sapling limbs
Start in my blood a wave of anger that
Breaks hotly on my eyes in spray that dims
Your hungry, haunted smile but cannot drown
The image of a child you bring to mind
Who might be mine: If ever, thin and brown,

137

She, too, must some day wait to find
Bread and forgiveness on the conquerors' way,
May they advance defeated—as today.

CHARLES EGLINGTON

Meeting

Confederates in this white field—
Our callings are allied—we will
Lie in rough comradeship until
Our flesh and spirit softly yield.

Then as your natural sympathy
Meets mine, the fierce caress
Is warm with sudden tenderness
And pacifies us utterly.

The unfamiliar room grows warm
As our heat radiates; the rain
Sobs like desire on the pane;
We rock together in the storm . . .

Until exhaustion stills us. First
You, falling suddenly asleep
On my slack arm, I plunging deep
Into the filled pool of my thirst,

And waking, later, find the chill
War-haunted city in the room:
And we, the spectres of its gloom,
Apart and yet together still.

Your naked breasts, untenderly
Loved, lie abandoned, but your face
Is tired and gentle with such grace
As I had never thought to see.

Madonna of the one-night bed,
Between revulsion and desire
I touch the limbs I have on hire
And stroke your tousled head.

But sleep divides us, so I muse:
Perhaps in every war it's we
Who in our love alone are free,
With least to win and least to lose.

CHARLES EGLINGTON

Arrival and Departure

The placid, rotted harbour has no voice
To bid departing travellers goodbye;
They, watching as land, sea and sky
Merge, are regretful of all things—the choice
That charts their steady course from day to day,
The port that lies behind, the one ahead,
The astrolabe of unrest that has led
Them north or south, but always the same way.

For strange each time the harbour reached, and far
The harbour that is home; each embarkation
Means farewell and every pilot-star

That winks the vessel to its destination
Burns briefly and the heart, anchored again,
Rocks on the tide, tugs at the anchor-chain.

GUY BUTLER

Cape Coloured Batman

As the slanting sun drowsed lazily
On the terraced groves of Tuscany
At last I found him, back to a trunk:
Nelson, my batman, the bastard, drunk.

On the grass beneath an olive tree
His legs splayed in a khaki V
And all his body, relaxed, at ease,
Head thrown back, while over his knees
Strumming the banjo his yellow hands
Stirred all his sorrow from four steel strands.

His melancholy cries from Hollywood
'Where the coyotes cry' or 'Lady be Good'
In that declining light awoke
A tenderness for the stupid bloke,
So happy his sorrow, so at ease
Strumming the strings across his knees.

No doubt a pirate Javanese
From Malacca Straits or Sunda Seas
Shaped those almond eyes of his:

A Negress from the Cameroons—
Bought for brandy, sold for doubloons—
Gave him a voice that wails and croons:

An eagle Arab trading far
From Hadramaut to Zanzibar
Left him a nose like a scimitar:

A Bush-girl from the Namaqua sands
Bequeathed him bird-like, restless hands
Stirring his sorrow from four steel strands:

While English, Dutch and Portuguese
Sick of biscuits and sodden cheese
Put in at the Tavern of the Seas,[1]

Northerners warm in the Southern night
Drank red Cape brandy, and got tight—
And left him a skin that's almost white.

This is the man the Empires made
From lesser breeds, the child of Trade
Left without hope in History's shade:

Shouldered aside into any old place,
Damned from birth by the great disgrace,
A touch of the tar-brush in his face.

Under pines, mimosas and mango trees
Strewn through the world lie men like these:
Drunk crooning voices, banjos on knees.

[1] The Tavern of the Seas: nickname for Cape Town.

He fell asleep in a vinous mist,
Star in his mouth, bottle in fist,
The desperate, maudlin hedonist.

But the pathos of the human race
Sainted his drunken, relaxed face;
And a warm dusk wind through the olive trees
Touched mute strings across his knees
With sorrows from the Seven Seas.

GUY BUTLER

Stranger to Europe

Stranger to Europe, waiting release,
My heart a torn-up, drying root
I breathed the rain of an Irish peace
That afternoon when a bird or a tree,
Long known as an exiled name, could cease
As such, take wing and trembling shoot
Green light and shade through the heart of me.

Near a knotty hedge we had stopped.
'This is an aspen.' 'Tell me more.'
Customary veils and masks had dropped.
Each looked at the hidden other in each.
Sure, we who could never kiss had leapt
To living conclusions long before
Golden chestnut or copper beech.

So, as the wind drove sapless leaves
Into the bonfire of the sun,
As thunderclouds made giant graves
Of the black, bare hills of Kerry,
In a swirl of shadow, words, one by one
Fell on the stubble and the sheaves;
'Wild dog rose this; this, hawthorn berry.'

But there was something more you meant,—
As if the trees and clouds had grown
Into a timeless flame that burnt
All worlds of words and left them dust
Through stubble and sedge by the late wind blown:
A love not born and not to be learnt,
But given and taken, an ultimate trust.

Now, between my restless eyes
And the scribbled wisdom of the ages
Black hills meet moving skies
And through rough hedges a late wind blows;
And in my palm through all the rages
Of lust and love now, always, lie
Brown hawthorn berry, red dog rose.

GUY BUTLER

Myths

Alone one noon on a sheet of igneous rock
I smashed a five-foot cobra's head to pulp;
Then, lifting its cool still-squirming gold

143

In my sweating ten separate fingers, suddenly
Tall aloes were also standing there,
Lichens were mat-red patches on glinting boulders,
Clouds were erupting white on the mountains' edge,
All, all insisting on being seen.
Familiar, and terribly strange, I felt the sun
Gauntlet my arms and cloak my growing shoulders.

Never quite the same again
Poplar, oak or pine, no, none
Of the multifarious shapes and scents that breed
About the homestead, below the dam, along the canal,
Or any place where a European,
Making the most of a fistful of water, splits
The brown and grey with wedges of daring green—
Known as invaders now, alien,
Like the sounds on my tongue, the pink on my skin;
Like my heroes, Jason, David, Robin Hood,
Leaving tentative footprints on the sand between
The aloe and the rock, uncertain if this
Were part of their proper destiny. Reading
Keats' *Lamia* and *Saint Agnes' Eve*
Beneath a giant pear tree buzzing with bloom
I glanced at the galvanized windmill turning
Its iron sunflower under the white hot sky
And wondered if a Grecian or Medieval dream
Could ever strike root away from our wedges of green,
Could ever belong down there
Where the level sheen on new lucerne stops short:
Where aloes and thorns thrust roughly out
Of the slate blue shales and purple dolorite.
Yet sometimes the ghosts that books had put in my brain

Would slip from their hiding behind my eyes
To take on flesh, the sometimes curious flesh
Of an African incarnation.

One winter dusk when the livid snow
On Swaershoek Pass went dull and the grey
Ashbushes grew dim in smudges of smoke,
I stopped at the outspan place to watch,
Intenser as the purple shades drew down,
A little fire leaping near a wagon,
Sending its acrid smoke into the homeless night.
Patient as despair, eyes closed, ugly,
The woman stretched small hands towards the flames;
But the man, back to an indigo boulder,
Face thrown up to the sky, was striking
Rivers of sorrow into the arid darkness
From the throat of a battered, cheap guitar.
It seemed that in an empty hell
Of darkness, cold and hunger I had stumbled on
Eurydice, ragged, deaf forever,
Orpheus playing to beasts that would or could not hear,
Both eternally lost to news or rumours of spring.

GUY BUTLER

David

You pure and nimble boy, like candle flame
Burning above the pebbled brook, you'll bring
Far more than wild doves tumbling down off wing:
Bronze-armoured giants shall crumple in your aim.

You shall be King, and Lion:
Out of your stripling flesh shall flower
Majesty, dominion, power
And the salt, white walls of Zion.

Bathsheba shall break you. Long histories
Shall hear your heart-beat leap and break in your rhyme:
O they'll forget your laws, your feats of arms,
But not the hour when with aching limbs
Dragging up steep stairs, your aimless eyes
Weep stones for all the Absaloms of Time.

GUY BUTLER

Pieta

Tremendous, marching through smashed buildings, trees,
A stream of bawdy bubbles from our lips.
Dog-eyed he stares from the ruin's lower steps,
Then frightened fingers flutter out to seize
His mother's dusty skirts. She lifts her eyes,
Straightens, flashes back at bay, and almost trips;
Then turns, goes out to him, him only, grips
His fear-blind head against her bending knees.

O silver cord, that, slipping so, unties
Compassion in her like a tidal sea,
You tighten round my throat, you strangle me
Till I could swear noon-darkness stuns the skies
Above a woman pierced beneath a tree
On whose black bough her one Son sweats and dies.

GUY BUTLER

Home Thoughts

I

Strange rumours gripped Olympus. Apollo's hand
Paused at its work, set plummet and rule aside;
Then glittering in clean-cut bronze he sped
To rout the brash disturbers of that peace
Which year by year had raised archaic Greece
Nearer his vision of the poised and planned.
O barbarous with drums, with dancing drums,
Amid a snarl of leopards through whose hide
Shimmer disastrous stars, the drunkard comes,
Black Dionysus roaring in his pride!

Ten thousand times they fought, wrestling before
Both gods and men; it seemed the very rocks
Watched those wild bouts among the barley shocks,
The brown vineyards, the dusty threshing floor.
If pressed Apollo side-slipped to the sun,
Striking his rival blind, while he in turn
Would slink instinctive into copses, run
Underground like roots, and hoot weird scorn
From his nocturnal world: but neither could
Conquer the force in which the other stood.

The spectacle gave poets double sight;
Their ears grew keen to catch at brightest noon
Rumours of drums; and dark, ecstatic night
Could wake with shafts not quivered in the moon.
At last, at Delphi, half in love with him,
Apollo gave the drunkard elbow room;

But though his pride of leopards purred, near tamed,
And he himself grew decorous, he might
Still breathe a deep, vibrating gloom
Round anything the Bright One named.

At length, when peasants through his autumn trance
Stirred slow pavanes for summer on soft drums
He cried aloud, (his leopards stretched their limbs):
Kill me, Apollo, or join the tragic dance!
Instead the Bright One watched: the flexing knees,
The raving, rending; heard the ecstatic crying;
But mirrored on his mind's white dancing floor
Dark dancers sighed and swayed like cypress trees
Around a man on whose defiant dying
Cracked clouds of knowing never moist before.

II

Why do I hanker homewards, falter?
Because in Arno's flood the stars
Cavort with neon signs, headlights of cars?
The Centaur, snapping its human halter,
Demolishes baroque façades;
The Great Bear runs amok
Among our maps, tugging the Pole awry;
O all things heave and buck
Since Dionysus slipped Apollo's guards
And let his leopards range the earth and sky!

Stupid of me to brood and cry
These barbarous confusions where
Triumphant marble effigies defy

The moody turmoils of the air;
But, as at home, I here discern
The predatory shade;
Asleep all day in ivy or that fern
Which smothers the balustrade
It sniffs the night and pads the cracked parterre
Between dry laurels and the shattered urn.

Man's task is to get such dark things clear.
Old Galileo, that empiricist
Through gothic tombs, antiphonies of psalms
Smuggled a serpent-sharp idea;
Smooth linen cordage looped in his swinging fist
Chilled the ascending stairs;
The sceptre-grasping ikons round the dome
Shook as his ape-like palms
Payed out that system-smashing metronome
Who jazztime spoilt the sweet waltz of the spheres.

Long years drifting through African dark
Bred dreams that I might find, once here
A burning beacon, a gyro-setting mark;—
That cord would ruck and tangle where
The rough stone of a leopard's bark
Ripples the scrub with fear.
What pendulum can trace the mind's unseen
Sharp arcs, its blind man's reach
Round knots of being that have never been
Subdued to slip through flaming hoops of speech?

Never so clearly have I known
That though the sharp mind's eye was made

To sever struggling shape from strangling shade
These shapes and shades cannot be mine.
O African creatures across this night
I glimpse in our primitive storm
Of thunder, whirlwind, mirage-twisted light
A lifted limb or glance
Which I might free, give consciousness and form
Dared I but stare into your furious dance!

III

Old Galileo's heirs can cite
How stubborn atoms may become
Open to change in unimpeded light,
Or round a rod of platinum
May curtsy, open arms and start
Dancing a different dance;
But the catalyst remains itself, apart,
Waits like a hermit there
Through dull khamseens of accident and chance
To set one crystal, get one colour clear.

These images at which I stare
Beneath such slow, myth-burdened stars,
Virgilian forests shedding mortal tears,
Might blind me in my native air.
Unless for some loved principle one strips,
As the desert fathers did,
The soul of gaudy accidents, and grips
A Mosaic serpent or rod
One's deepest cries come from Egyptian lips
Blowing dead bubbles on a Red Sea flood.

IV

I have not found myself on Europe's maps,
A world of things, deep things I know endure
But not the context for my one perhaps.
I must go back with my five simple slaves
To soil still savage, in a sense still pure:
My loveless, shallow land of artless shapes
Where no ghosts glamorize the recent graves
And every thing in Space and Time just is:
What similes can flash across those gaps
Undramatized by sharp antithesis?

I boast no quiet catalytic wand
Nor silently swinging, tell-tale pendulum
To civilize my semi-barbarous land;
A clearer love is all that I bring home:
Little, yet more than enough. Apollo, come!
O cross the tangled scrub, the uncouth ways,
Visit our vital if untamed abysm
Where your old rival in the lustrous gloom
Creates a different dance, a brand-new rhythm
To spell this dumb earth's agony and praise.

Perhaps among the shrubs and pebbles of this land
Profiles not worn by centuries of use,
Shapes, textures, new to your subtle hand,
Sounds, likely to startle the blasé muse,
Perhaps the old dynamic shade will come,
Nervous, breathless, avoiding your vision's range:
But if, if only you will watch, will wait
You'll kindle in that lightning interchange
When thick clouds crack and to a thunder's drum
Fall crystal words, dancing, articulate.

RUTH MILLER

Fruit

These were the distant fruits of a garden childhood:
Yellow fluff on the hard astringent quince—
Finger-scratched to smooth small streets and lanes;
Cornelian-coloured ball of pomegranate,
Split in shining cups of pirate rubies
Set each against each like bee-cells in white silk;
Figs that we shredded, pulpy soft and purple,
Throwing aside the dry and skeined imposters,
Their milkflesh stained with russet short-cut threads.

Sunday fruit was silver-bought. But these
Grew in the garden, formed a roadside hedge,
Concealed us from the coinage of the world.
Amongst the quince, the fig, the pomegranate
We hid away with glossy greensprung secrets;
Lay quiet and heavy, sweet with an edge of bitter
Under the lazy heat, the languorous season:
Breathless to be plucked and by love consumed.

RUTH MILLER

Honey

The helicopter bee fines down
His motor to a midget drone.
The creamfurred throat engulfs him. Soon
His legs grow pantaloons of gold.

His thousand brothers sing and thrust
Their piston legs, their pinion gauze,
Blind to the plundering soft raid
On catacombs of murmuring halls.

Now cool long jars gleam with the taste
Of amber hours suavely stolen
From summer swooning in the heat;
Till smooth and pale, and pale and golden,
There slides like bliss upon the tongue
A bawd's red kiss, a drudge's song.

RUTH MILLER

Fundisi[1]

The sacred lake of Fundisi is an eye of moonstone,
A cyclops eye in the green forehead of the hills;
Nightlidded, darklashed with the clashing reeds,
It weeps no tears.

Long ago it was crimsoned—Oh, keep away from the reeds!
Those newly born, they made such a little plash.
Only the mother shrieked, but silently,
And wept no tears.

Three rivers sew their silver threads, soft-sliding
Into the eye of Fundisi, its blank white stare,
Filling it, scalloped and scooped to the ductless rim;
For it sheds no tear.

[1] Fundisi, in the Northern Transvaal, is considered sacred by the local tribes because three rivers run into it, with no visible exit.

Deep, dark and deep in the green flesh of the earth,
Underground, brackish, the bounteous exodus goes.
The tribes perceived only the infinity of the finite,
And fell to tears.

Oh, keep away, keep away from the reeds at the edge of
    Fundisi,
At night, when the clash of their blades is a rattle like spears;
For is it not we who are rivers, engorging the cyclops,
And weeping, like it, concealed, subterranean tears?

RUTH MILLER

The Floating Island

Down the glutted river's throat
Jut the jagged trunks of trees,
Giddily the bubbles float;
The dead drowned buck have wounded knees.
The basket nests ooze mud in sodden trees.

Swirling in a giddy gyre
Down the brown Zambesi flood
Comes an island—torn entire
With tendon reeds and brackish blood,
Prised from its moorings in the silent mud,

Bearing on its swinging arc
A herd of buck, alive, aground,
With anguished eyes, their wet flanks dark
With sweat. The water gabbles round.
Their sucking hoofprints moon the mud with sound.

154

The sliding scenery repeats
The gliding greenery of fear.
A newborn buck gropes for the teats;
Green to terror, he does not hear
The lipping tongues around his mother's feet.

Head back, flat, with seashell horns
Against the wind the leader strains.
Around him lean the does and fawns:
They can remember summer rains—
But not like these. Not these obliterated plains.

Do they smell the tumbling doom
Scarved in silken spray that slides
To the falling ledge, that looms
But one nightfall on? Their sides
Bulge and flatten. Their eyes darken and grow wide.

Along the gorged Zambesi swims
In a slow insensate dance
Frieze of buck with dervish limbs
Frozen in a dreamer's trance.
Anarchy has leapt beyond mischance.

A nightfall on the Smoke that Thunders[1]
Will spring to gulf their leaping sides.
Wrenched from our continent, we blunder
And lacking weather-sense for guide
Our green uncharted islands sink in ravelled floods, blind-eyed.

[1] The Smoke that Thunders: African name for the Victoria Falls.

DAVID WRIGHT

Seven South African Poems

I

Each time I return to Johannesburg it is summer,
And clouds hang with black the stage of the sky,
So I perceive the auditors prepared for tragedy,
Ready for lightning, where a harp of thunder

Leans towards Magaliesberg. Does my childhood
Lie before those mountains, where Pretoria
Veils her white façades with jacaranda
Below their shoulders? From Orange Grove

I'd look all the morning at the distance laid between,
The bare areas, undeveloped altitudes,
And plant their furlongs with imagined woods
To be grown in the fields between Magaliesberg and my home.

Over them stoop and bend the throats of summer
Each time I return to Johannesburg. Over them
I see and hear a portentous requiem
Performed, at each return, by my native weather,

For burial of the closing distances.
The scale grows less. I see the mountains near
My home at each return, dwindle and wither
The imagined woods as death to birth advances.

Mr. Ellis, the owner of the Orange Grove
Hotel, in the suburbs of my native city,
Going after Lobengula's buried ivory,
Could never discover its guarded alcove.

Though the aasvogel and the lion's head
He took back, to stuff in the sockets of their eyes
Imitation anger with glass irises,
Might have delighted with novelty the dead

Man sewn in the skin of two oxen. Lobengula,
Whose continent has no memory, a sleeping
Moody appeasable spirit, is keeping
A long silence and two waggons of ivory.

As over the Limpopo and Magaliesberg
To the Fish River, on each Dingaan's Day,
Lifts a tinkle of drums for the broken assegai,
For the tribes broken in Johannesburg;

Lobengula's body by the river M'Lindi
Dries, and with the bones of Moselekatse, Rhodes
Lies royal, Ulodzi, upon the Matoppos,
Romantic emperor and parish Alexander

Keeping his diamond in his cheek; Oom Paul[1]
Rests in Pretoria, the Bible to a thumb
Acquainted with labour, and the premier waggon
Spanning liberty over the Orange and the Vaal;

[1] Paul Kruger, last President of the Transvaal.

By the banks of Umgusa, the Orange Grove
Hotel proprietor on a final safari
Approaches the tribute the last Matabele,
Lobengula, exacted with terror and love.

III

My grandfather was an elegant gentleman
Who trod behind an ox-waggon's wheels in his youth
Four hundred miles to Kimberley from Port Elizabeth,
To resuscitate the family fortune.

His love affair with money lasted a long time.
In my childhood I best remember
His glass-panelled car and European chauffeur,
And dignity in a cricket pavilion;

Or when in gardens imitating England
He in a morning-coat between two ladies
Walked. I was afraid to recognize
My father's father, and kept my distance.

Nothing became my grandfather so much as his age.
Impoverished and living in a single room,
He kept his grace and distinguished costume,
Imposing on distress an unstooping carriage.

The lady left him, but he took his congé
Like a gentleman. The old colonial
Never allowed a merely personal
Regret pour a poison in the ear of memory.

158

My favourite myth was the legend of Dr. Livingstone
With linen, salvation, beads and love in his hand,
Searching the continent for Herodotus' fountains,
And leaving after his death his heart and his guts behind.

The parson who recorded his defeat in dialectics
By an African wizard, going without a whip or a gun
In his hand, to the rivers and the inland lakes,
Among the savage and terrified, came to no harm.

Seeing the Zambesi roll like a leaf below
Him, and the valley of black humankind
Rise like an arm to religion and to their
Peace, the kindly and self-disciplined

Man in the end left their shackles forgotten,
Heard not any more the natural cry
Of the chained river. For more than freedom
He respected the curiosity

That once to glimpse the divided hill
Where the four sources of the Nile shape variously,
Was a last passion, and the final
Burial of his will and energy.

In which prayer dying, David Livingstone
Passed, and those whom he could not save
Carried his bones to Zanzibar and England,
But kept his heart and innards in their proper grave.

In nineteen twenty-eight my father's office boy
Died, and his mother followed, weeping,
Black as a widow, the hearse and tripping
Horses to a boneyard dressed with snow.

In Eloff Street an automobile knocked him down.
So he said goodbye to ledgers, it was goodbye
To the Stock Exchange, and adieu eternally
To the firm of O. D. Wright & Son.

Over the crossing angels the pepper trees
Droop, and the cloches of Eternal Flowers
Smudge with dust. The shaking towers
Of white mines muttering where he is

Extract the gold. My father's office boy
Who lies in Johannesburg under the sun
In marble companies, lies in silence shaking down
A quilt of sleep on each man's memory.

VI

For Roy Campbell

My countryman, the poet, wears a Stetson;
He can count his enemies, but not his friends,
A retired soldier living in Kensington,
Who limps along the Church Street to the Swan.

Horses and bulls, the sable and impala,
Sparkle between his fingers, and a sun
That sleeps and rises from the Indian Ocean
Gongs the images of his passion.

He never loved liberty for her name,
Or wept on the disastrous ashes of Guernica,
But he fought for her where he could find her,
Knowing she was not lying in a newspaper column,

But bound, still bound in the aboriginal fall
From Eden and of Adam. His ancestors who came
Out of the eighteenth century and Scotland
Taught him to have no truck with the liberal.

Horses and bulls, the sable and impala,
Thunder between his fingers; as they run,
He hears another thunder in the sun,
Time and the sea about Tristan da Cunha.

VII

Now I remember Cabo da Boa
Esperança, which I left one day in autumn
On the Balmoral Castle, to never return:
Farewell to Table Mountain, St James and Saldhana

Bay where a boy I became aware of Eden;
Farewell to behind them the stairs of Africa,
To her rivers of willow, and the local kinema,
The legless kaffir on the Town Hall pavement;

To the cycling boys with candles in their hands
Racing the curfew in the dark at Orange Grove,
To a European tram bellowing down to Norwood,
And the grand processions of the yoked ox waggons.

As on a morning my great-grandfathers came
In sight of Algoa, of the roller-pounded sands,
Her lion-crouched woods and silver-hatted mountains,
One autumn, I left on an autumn afternoon

On a marriage bed of waters where the Indian
And the Atlantic ocean gently meet;
There saw at last, from a liner's after-deck,
The last of Africa divide the horizon.

DAVID WRIGHT

From *A Voyage to Africa*

I

Adamastor, whom Camoens and the sea
Invented, was a giant who, we are told,
With Achilles' future mother wished to lie,
But met with a fool's mate colder than the snow.
To become a seamark over Table Bay

Because the young lady turned him into stone.
You, my dear Adamastor, I invoke
(A myth, but the first immigrant European)
To come out from under your white tablecloth
And, if you like, to bless the following poem.

Your outlook, bony and magnificent, leans
Upon waves fanning towards the deader pole,
The irreconcilable and married oceans,
With a real authority, superb and full,
With visions of a continent of penguins.

On your right, like gods or angels in a play,
Some Portuguese seamen, followed by some Dutch,
With sails and guns made their romantic entry
(But read Buffon upon female Hottentots)
And thus began South African history;

While on your left, or sinister, side there sleep
The bones of Dingaan's brother, and of Dingaan—
May their siesta prove unpleasant, and not light,
That nothing may discommode the present plan
Of many blacks labouring to make a white.

I, who left England upon St. Lucy's day
And longest night, am undertaking to tell
In verses of a voyage to Africa;
And you, Adamastor, although somewhat dull
And deaf, must help to sustain me if I fly;

For I, born in fields you turn your back upon,
Lying between Sahara and Cape Aguilhas,
May legitimately claim to be your son.
You'd have preferred the fathering of Achilles—
Acquiesce in your destiny of a stone!

As quiet has been my fortune and your gift,
We should collaborate. Let me now begin.
At Northampton, in a high school for the deaf,
I was reading about Adonais, when
A whole Europe was engaged in peace,

Seesawing like a hesitant suicide
Before the act. O world of my adolescence
Not altogether entitled to regard,

But less completely black than the midwinter's
Night at Tilbury when I waited for the tide

And the hemispheres that now keep war on ice
Lay asleep, folded in a total gloom
As Thames, bearing down his comments to a rise
Of waters from a deep and shallow ocean,
Carried what fell so easily from my eyes.

That slumbering island with some stars disposed
Possessed me. While the river, seaborne, moved
Lost in a night's profoundest and longest shade,
On either side of the water slept or grieved
Those that made and loved me that I loved and made.

So, loving island, towering west and north,
She encompassed with sad massive arms my sleeping.
What is a man's birthplace? Where the man came forth.
Not where his embryo, dangerously leaping,
Arrives naked at an accidental hearth.

In no other way I acknowledged my home
Than by knowing her immense, and as a bride
Exhausted and fulfilled, when at her groin
I lay that night near and distant to her side
And left her in darkness to embark alone. . . .

II

. . . Here I was born. And here, like asparagus,
The small aspirations claw a higher sky
With commodities of an unchanged progress
Towards the exhaustion of the means to die.
Black, here, is the actual colour of distress:

Black as an adder to fear and to comfort.
The great American saloon cars blast by
Illustrious. As the summer ends the drought,
Summer its pandemonium gathers high
In purple cumuli over Magaliesberg.

An immaterial default will not perturb
Above undermining and minotaur caverns
The city which, without centre but a suburb,
Dishonoured by the distances and heavens,
Apparently proliferates and prospers.

By day the rocks, inhuman, flash from their hill
Or sweat with rain above this mortifying
City which I must inhabit; these appal;
O human city in a wilderness lying,
Holy about you night and lightning fall.

Here I was born, and here I am come back
To meet the consolation she provides.
That glittering white sierra, where neglect
Perpetuates an empire which she denies,
Swans on the silent border of a lake

Where thunder hangs, and so surrounds and threatens
With an accusation of rejected dust.
Let not rejection be a consolation.
Lose but not loose me, and I am not lost
To glory on the mines of desolation

That, thrown up by a Witwatersrand, outlie
The city where I was born, Johannesburg,
Balanced between the plateaux of a sky

And the deep ground; miserable as superb,
Common as divine, and like humanity.

Where by Orange Grove mimosas are cut down
And some orchards fallen to the building plots,
I abide by what proves to be not my home
Part of this journey. Let Moselekatse
Nek notched to the Magaliesberg mountain plume

Keep tally if I hear the goldfinches call
Above green cedar branches upon whose trees
I felt, first, a purgatorial silence fall,
Second, the consolation that always is
That all is well and shall console us all.

III

How gentle, courteous, and noble is nature
Whose beasts, when visible, appear dumb and good,
And whose prospects, munificent but pure;
Or she is cruel if that should be the mood,
May be dressed in or divested of allure.

A mirror more perfect than any of glass
She is: when looked in, the looker sees a shape
Of his emotion, and of what really was
There, looking in; of an angel or an ape.
If her mountains lean towards beguiling us—

In whom, once, we saw a visage of our fright,
Though long ago, and in another country,
Whereas today they flatter us with their height—
O nature, mirror or mishandled pantry,
Or medicine, goddess, enemy, what you like—

I love you, and knowing whom I really love
I find it difficult not to love you more;
Either in a city's confines, at one remove,
Or when I, travelling past in train or car,
Touch the innocence your wildernesses prove.

As for the human spectators there on show
(Whose stink of worry, effectively overcome
By a scent of steel and petrol, does not now
Terrify to a stampede the herds of horn)
Become beasts by virtue of machines, they go

By Sabi in the Kruger National Park
Where the lions, mewing from Pretorius Kop
And light-bummed impala, poised as a photograph,
Live easy as in an Eden, have no hope;
Content with joy infects with joy their dark.

Cropping under rocks depending for their fall,
Sunlit, the prelapsarian creatures move;
In their incommunicable selfish toil
They praise what made them with no need to love
Or ever to manifest that praise at all,

As we are led, by what I am now aware
Is guilt of loving not enough, to beg pardon,
Embarrassed by overmuch of love and care
And so excluded from the encircling garden,
In learning and in the laud of what moves there.

The hairy and stupid beasts that have no troubles
Beyond rinderpest and acts of God, increase.
A hippo, lulled by water, is snoring bubbles

While lion beside the zebra loll at peace;
Scavenging from heaven, an aasvogel wobbles;

And intelligent babooneries alone
Who peer from behind their thrones of boulders, pierce
The simple human disguise of a machine,
Avoiding the direction of eyes and ears
And of a curiosity like their own.

Here, virginal, without a memory, or
Regret, and balancing like a week's wash
Her clouds of summer over what cause affords,
The thorn-appointed veld unlids that face
The kraals of Umgungundhlovu[1] rose towards,

But with not easily felt neutrality
Wields the indifference of a regard
That, deafer than a wilderness or the sky,
Seems yet to have seen where each black beast and guard
Makes shift, at night, in secret, towards its day.

About to fly of a midnight to England
I half turn, affected as a lover, while
Exiled I quit what seems a native ground,
Engage, already exiled, on an exile
With a half mad Europe to my northern hand;

Which to inherit, flying far and over
Johannesburg—above whose black defiles
The street lamps burn as I again remember
(O delectable in dark, luminous under hills)
That every farewell is in fact for ever—

[1] The royal seat of Dingaan.

168

A leaning plane's wing lifts me swiftly further.
In her long gown of evening she drags away,
And far lights flutter to a broad tiara.
Obscure, below, prodigious, and gothic, lie
The expanses galloping to a grand Sahara.

JOHN PETER

Reading Tolstoy

Leisure the serfs will not forget
To banquet, love, and play
And which meanwhile their straits abet
Day after cordial day:
To draw life up upon the hook
More opulent than ours and yet
I find my childhood in this book
Two lives, three worlds away.

Those tough dynastic families
Exchange no further call,
Their lightning-charred anatomies
Will not be at the ball.
My nursegirl used to tell me when
Thunder began to shake the trees
It was a time to pray and then
Wait for the sky to fall.

JOHN PETER

Cypress

Seventeen years ago, the sun so glaring
It paled the eating flame invisibly
I burned love letters under such a tree
Equably, undespairing.

The silence lingered overhead
Tolerant of petty apostasies
Sober funereal trees
As Virgil said.

This other cypress
Menaces the hot shade
Like an old assegai's discoloured blade
Offers its stinging kiss.

No use affecting unconcern
Looking the other way
In this sun-darkened domicile today
Whose letters shall we burn?

JOHN PETER

Christmas on Three Continents

Snow-masked and bell-bewitched the village
Supports a stratus architrave,

Frost decorates the sweeps of tillage
Holly the corbels of the nave,
Their magic now as Christian
As crusade's cross or barbican.

A whip of wind larrups the city
Etching ice on eave and sill,
Lays bare a world so bleak of pity
Its god seems hewn of frozen steel;
In heated stores a haunted crowd
Clutch at the comforts still allowed.

Here too the seasonal extremes
Volunteer a harsh embrace
But here divinity beseems
An aboriginal sweating face
Indifferent to love or hate
Incomprehensible to placate.

JOHN PETER

Estrangement

I

Storm-sudden summer filled the dongas[1] with thunder
Fawn watercliffs with frothcrests running wild
Snatching at likkewaans[2] and thornbranch plunder
And an occasional child

[1] Donga: watercourse.   [2] Likkewaan: iguana, a large lizard.

While Gabriel Oak went softly across a snowscape
Bland with the bells of an impassive steeple
Human inquietude forfeiting shape
Until mere people

Lost all identity except as shifting values in
Soft glooms of light under the winter woods
Where an inscrutable season could begin
To sift its moods

Nor was he recorded sipping the bitter draught
Of rainwater staled in the leaf-elbows of aloes
After an afternoon staring along a rifleshaft
Into the wind's bellows

Nor mouthing the resinous softness dissolving
Of sunwhite mimosa-gum like tepid ice
Hung on trees with brittle black bark involving
Unnamed varieties of lice

But piling hay like gold below hills like pillows
Or ploughing where pale riparian mist scented the view
For he was also Ash and Elm and pollarded willows
A herald too

Summoning us through nights when Southern Cross and
        Plough
Vied in the rigging for domination of the sky
Their rivalry a tilt of the planet that now
Perceptibly

Steadied itself under our keel and without guile
Proffered a rim of pasture above the line to port
Green as a larch in snow and low as a stile
Profuse as a thought

Of history which soon became feasible and small
Enclosed between the shires and cities
Or angles of a sunlit wall.

II

Annoyance became insurgent and then defaulted
To any force soliciting the eye
Masonry snugly crouched or superbly vaulted
Across the trajectory of a sigh

Lifting and lapsing like larks who spun a floss
Diaphanous of notes to quicken the air
Settling in turn like thistledown into silence or across
The woodland where

Squirrels and jays cavorted and posed and celandine
Startled the turf and primroses and wild violets came
With the modesty and precision of small machines
And all the same

It was unauthentic and dubious like the asphalt paths
In parks where nursemaids no longer strolled
For Time had overtaken them and cut his swaths
There and in Gabriel's fold

So that anachronism and disavowal
Blurred in the mind and set us to explore
Our vision turning curious and dual
Reported that it saw

Privilege four feet tall and rather tight
And Art caressing a crucifix and a rump
Learning grown rancorous and polite
As a hunchback to his hump

173

A peasantry quick as their ferrets to molest
And navvies in a cinema in tears
Saw too that the blue distances we'd crossed
Were latitudes of years

Across which the trustworthy rifles of our youth
Were lifted now like a malison or a fence
Shutting us out in the vacancy of truth
And the present tense

Where bare feet groped in a donga-bed of drought
Marred with the forking thorns of our self-pities
The litter and trash of doubt.

JOHN PETER

Heart's Desire

Gathering, tall, a wave in a vicious sea
Tension smoked and fell forward, spilling loose.
After the acid lights, fear like a sluice
Narrowing, screams of silence, repartee
Of guilt and vindication, placidly
She made her last decision. A recluse
Was shut within the white walls of a truce,
The reassuring clean infirmary.

Having achieved it, though, it disappeared.
Stertorous clocks fell silent while the years
Blinked on her eyelids, now incapable
Of vision, vanity, or even tears.
Sometimes she heard an untranslatable
Snigger, and thought the unseen concord sneered.

ANNE WELSH

Sight

A shine and shock
Are scarlet lilies
By sun-dazzled waters.
Storm-bloom on hills,
Rock-sparkle or bright glass—
Each colour is a cock
That crows of glory.

Sun sprays new fibres
On leaf-cool collections,
And golden butterflies
Dance on a dusty surface.
Rivers are pliant light
Or stanchions taut for sun.
Grasses, ivory, or rose,
Stones, apricot, or red
Smoulder to pale miles overhead.

Out of the crowded valley's colour
Single call-notes trumpet as I pass,
Till eyes are strutting peacocks,
And sharp mosaics
Block out distance
Where no fronds wave.

In glittering valleys
Shine is more lucid than an argument,
Horizons make an arbitrary ring,
And this closed-circuit for the eyes
Sets all the roundelays.

Distance is silent—
It is beyond the sight.
O mountains not seen, can I recognize,
Or ever discover your colours
When articulate trumpets are missing?

ANNE WELSH

Victoria Dancing

Victoria was a little girl; daughter of an African mother and a Coloured father, she was brought up partly in the home of her parents' white employers, who treated her as one of the family. She was quite untouched by 'colour consciousness'. She skipped beside a bus queue.

Step-stream pavement bears
Victoria, dragon-fly dancing,
Eyes coal-shining.
In dusk she sparkles
For race-taut strangers.

She is child out of season,
Drought brought lily
Unexpected of the dust.
Limp lights focus
On her sharp green thrust.

Firefly-inquisitive, Victoria
Dances, a small flame leaping
On race-cold faces.
But none of her beckoning
Brings a new season.

Privately fire-green, Victoria
Dances through seasons of ashes
Foul to the light limb—
Under our leafless hearts
Finds a withered world.

Will the seasonless embers,
The ash-bedded amber and rose,
Accompany green,
And Victoria, sapling-uncertain,
Be doubtful of death in the ash?

ANNE WELSH

The Body's Eye

Tin-bright and whistle-sharp the world occurs
Round walls that are not walls but entrances.
This feather touching of a coloured wind
Strokes its way in past all the whimpering curs
Of my complaints. I am out of the sleep
That closes day-doors for private basking
Under imagined suns the mind prefers.

To-day is stalwart, sun-high, kestrel-high,
Light as the beating wings that keep my time
Hovering. As pivot earth turns trees
The roots and branches of the body's eye
Are turned, and the immediate ochre
Of the grass keeps pace. I am not absolute
Not yet done with, while I am body's eye.

For this occasion dark's identified—
The pit, the desert of completed night,
And that primaeval pool of slattern grey
We can look on and never find a tide.
Only the turning world is incomplete,
Morning and evening fresh for moving pain,
And for raw colours where the old have died.

Small in the shade of cliffs, children admire
A world where birds are not dead leaves, and flowers
Are brighter than the blooms' veiled follower
Of shadowed colour. Love's red ashes fire
Children harder. From scarlet kilns they cry
For lucid looking, and for earth imaged
In earth, to meet the flesh of their desire.

Pluck from the manifold bright bars of light
And order chaos. Lift flashes from
That turbulent dark, whose noisy wind
Flexes a passage through the cells of night.
Each bar's an image, single point of law,
Stamped with the seal of gold significance;
Each bar compresses hydra-headed sight.

But soon I am barricaded, soon sun
Retreats from this safe area. Images
Cultivated like young tender plants
Turn fossil cold, and the pale order won
Out of welter dark dies in the dark.
Here there are only words obscuring words,
Till image and the earth have fused to one.

Now in this blue occasion of the sky
Light glances through the skin, and tent-wide bones
Open for quick acknowledgement of day
Housed in the spires of chimneys, and in high
Unsucculent pastures of the beardless wind.
Now seasons overrule the calendars—
Image is put to question by the eye.

Death or dishevelment we are constrained
By this one Universe to look beyond
Images crusted with time's accretions.
The head of sight is caught on our craned
Necks, and tall worlds lean against the eye
Till images are sprung within the bones
To make the bones of light; and world's regained.

ROY MACNAB

Child of the Long Grass

No one will remember
Now they've set the grass burning,
How high grew these curtains for love
In the Summer. Then Msasa was blazing
Red beacons for lovers and I was conceived,
Child of the long grass.

Oh my mother, my father,
Now Winter divides you
And leafless Msasa is loverless too,

179

O why have you left me, flower of your bearing,
Now that they're breaking
My cradle in flame?

ROY MACNAB

Majuba Hill

On the craggy mountain-top the mist
Held a redcoat army in its fist.
Beaten by arrogance and the sun,
They'd dragged their last uncaptured gun,

To make a fortress of the hill
And watch all night from the citadel.

The creatures of the mist, the sheep
Sniffed round the red men in their sleep,
The only sentries still awake
Who heard the yielding branches break.

For the five-day sleepless sentry stood
And snored at his post above the wood,
While down upon the stirring plain
The night brought up its Dunsinane.

The moon went skulking from the sky
And hid its face as the wood passed by,
A few score Boer and bearded trees
Scaling the mountain on their knees.

The dawn rose up from an angry bed,
Drew back the shroud from the mountain-head,
And sent the sun out over the stones
To gnaw at the sleeping soldiers' bones.

The soldiers sleeping in the sun
Could never know what the night had done,
How bitter were the blazing noons,
The defeat in dust of proud dragoons.

Only the nibbling goat and the sheep
Saw how remote were the dead asleep.

ROY MACNAB

The Settler

Torn from his country bed,
Of green lanes and a sultry stream,
By war and its attendant dead,
He cast off custom for a new dream,

Blocked up the tunnel of his return,
Where the stone pages of history lay
Scorched and scattered in no hallowed urn
And no sun danced on the blackened day,

When love had been lost on ghostly towers,
Known in innocence and without shame,
Where the past ages had strewn flowers
For the brides acquiring his honoured name,

And a grave untouched by the tarnished cup
Of memories' dregs and the tang of wine
Not to be tasted again, nor borne up
With joy from the mind; already the sign

Of death familiar in battle and churchyard,
Stood over his family fame and the gate
Closed on their fortunes, the sepulchre's card
Left to the scholar to fulminate.

Put paid at last to the ghostly tower,
He dug new life from a stranger's land,
Thrilled to the plough and primitive power
And buried his sorrow in the Buddha's hand.

O not to follow in the ancestral way,
But to dive in first to the rippleless pool,
Shorn of the shackles and the old decay,
Such was his freedom and the tool

That blistered his touch and carved
Out of the stone and the sorrow
Of the age, the hope-starved
Day, pages of an uncut morrow.

ROY MACNAB

From *The Man of Grass*[1]

II

India became his jasmined youth, Goa
Prescribed the limits of decision,
But in all those years Africa sang
Like fever in his ears, and Sofala
Laughed in the corridors of ambition.

Now like a star it draws him westward;
Black the sky and bleak the seas
Threaten the coast of Mozambique,
And the Arabs with their seamen's eye
Marvel at the priest upon his knees.

Creation reconceived in fury
Flung out of the well of the sea
Mobile mountains that mocked the planned
Arrangement of water and land,
With wind and rain and storm.

Torment of water broke and buckled
Bows of the zambucko, the seamen's skill
Torn on the side of the whirling hill
Of the gale and hope lay wracked
On the aching rope and the sail.

[1] The Man of Grass: name given by Monomatapa to Gonzalo da
Silveira, a Portuguese Jesuit, martyred in what is now Rhodesia in 1561.

Only Gonzalo the priest went undismayed
On his knees by the sailors and prayed:
Domine, Domine, Domine,
Salva nos, salva nos, perimus,
Domine, salva nos, perimus.
And the seas stop; the lashing
Winds stop at the place of his passion.

III

The sea releases me. Sand
Of Africa insinuates warmth,
Into my faltering feet. Land
Of my vision smiles in the sun.

I see beginning and end in the same place,
Mind and matter integrate
Here on the stone's white face,
In the circle of sacrament.

Among heathens I begin benediction
Of baptism, break bread and repeat
The ritual of wine, dispel the fiction
Of the sorcerer's bones.

Now the wind among mangroves
Takes up the service, polite palms
Whisper, praises and voices
Are lifted up loudly with psalms.

Yet the day dies with the sigh
Of trees and the low uneven moan
Of seas of my past—and at last
I and my God are alone.

V

Appointed I came a missionary
To Mtoko, lifted were the black faces
And voices for my coming and I
Spreading among the stone of bare places
Seed of my journey.

Laid open were the gates of Monomotapa,
And I for the siege of the infidel master;
Yet vultures I see that peck at the sky,
Above the clayhut kingdom disaster
Flying at the height of summer.

Winds whisper behind my back
Like cold rumours, no friend
I see in the transitory stare
Of the children, in their eyes only my end,
Only their innocence.

Yet here is my happiness, hunger
Of exile, the binding chain
Of earth and existence. I welcome the bond
Yet dream of deliverance, the brain
Unsheathed in the act of death.
O soon, soon the act of deliverance.

Line of my journey bends under the axe,
Disintegrates into the red
Of the earth, is the alien seed
Of another year's harvest; O the thread
Of my living begs for the breaking.

. . . Now is the day done and my journey;
I remember at Coimbra the first signpost
And now where the river turns I stand
Counting the roads I have come,
Accumulating the burdens of age,
Adding the sickness of life, the filth
Of the world. O in these two hands
All India's refuse, all Africa's
Contamination. O take me now
From decay's dark dunghill.

O you who are workers among forests,
Knowing the touch and the taste of trees,
Choose now the wood for my going,
Stout branches of crucifixion, firm logs
To feed the fire of the stake
Or the planting of the high gallows.

O I am the ready wood for your axes,
The sharpening block for your knives.
Then take me now while the spirit is strong,
And my body bending like a bough
In the storm of fates, my limbs
To be leaves scattered on winter winds,
O take me now, O take me now,
Now that I am willing.

L. D. LERNER

Senchi Ferry: Gold Coast

With a wet slap the red road hit the plain,
Spattering trees. A river lurked along this country, called
The fishermen, bright eyed and hungry, and boys,
And lilting women under a water-pot,
And sullen lovers hearing its dull
Insistent beating between their hearts.
The road swept downhill, changing gear,
Dogs fowls and cattle shrill wings beating fled,
Below, the river waited for the splash.

Now a calm crossing plies; the stream is hushed,
Impatient thousands scramble on its back.
It only sighs, and shrivels; nudges eddies;
Gives a dry laugh, helps wash the offered bodies:
Brown white streaked with soap their backs convulse,
Dive glide shed their white coats in the oily stream.

The fisherman tugs at his cast net.
It interlaced the water, crisply patterned the stream.
He tugs, calling
Here come up, quick come up, come; this way, come this way.
    Shun
The rocks' clutch, sand's suck,
Sea muttering which the water bears.
Don't go there, the sea is far away.
Far the shouting surf, whose call
The electric waters of the stream relay.

A lorry snarled. The wind had caught the crowd,
Flung it aloft, and sent it spinning down.
It beat around the scaly back;
Athwart it foaming slid the metalled sides,
Shed catching fingers, as the wide mouth bit the air:
The lorry lashed its tail and shot away.

A stream flows over the stream. Man knows
His way and his destination. Each carries
An enamel jug, or a carpet grubby with kneeling,
A bowl of rice, or the knowledge of being expected.
All men flow knowing, yet all men drift;
Men hear a call like the cry of the surf
Under the lorry's snarl, the boys, the women's voices,
—The tread of cattle, stepping to the market,
Their tired hooves tired hooves thudding on the road.

L. D. LERNER

The Desert Travellers

'*They travel in the desert as it were upon the sea, having
guides to pilot them by the stars or rocks in the desert.*'
(*An old account of travel in the Sahara*)

As it were upon the sea. Under the wind's hand
Waves wander and confuse the traveller,
Who, competent on land,
Strays thirsting here:
Letting his body drift across the sand
As it were upon the sea.

I, Ibn Battuta, scholar of Arabia,
Ambassador, guest of the Sultan, friend of many monarchs,
Went seeking Mansa Musa, ruler of Mali.
Went through the desert, and found the land of black men.
I lost myself with a troop of traders seeking
Gold from the shifting empires. Time passed by.
Southwards from Sigilmassa they sailed with salt,
Over the dry sea, after the gold of Guinea.
One century we found the silent traders,
Who left their gold, and stole the salt by dark.
They would not speak. Their tongues were parched with pride.
Pride in man's useless dust.

> Around us on the sand the sun is strewn.
> The shifting stars deceive the erring eye,
> Lie low behind a shifted dune,
> Or stray in the parched sky.
> Through this uncharted bland serenity
> The takshif leads us, sailing silently
> As it were upon the sea.

The takshif who led us was almost blind, and rode
The roll and pitch of his grinning camel well;
Each mile stopped suddenly dead,
Smelling a handful of sand, and said
That way, it's that way: riding by smell
On the gliding camel.
('I have ridden among these dunes that lie
Loosely on my sight as the light fades.
I have ridden among the corridors of air,
The cloudy palaces, the moving shades.
Have ridden, and I can tell
That way the grains are split by the sun, while here

The sand has withered like my eyes, and there
The setting sun has dragged the desert smooth.'
The takshif, riding on his pitching camel,
Riding by smell.)

I, Ibn Battuta, scholar, saw many marvels,
Passing through many ages, sailing the desert.

L. D. LERNER

14 July 1956

The rockets bubble upward and explode;
The colours scale the slopes of sky and fall.
A few look up; somebody says 'That's all';
No sigh or shudder rises from the crowd.
They must be here because they want to be.

We chatter to the crowd in French and nods;
Shake hands, and pick up children; claim that we
Are also equal, free and brotherly.
The troubled sky suggests the wrath of gods.
'Always the same,' a woman says, and goes.

The fireworks scatter to the ground and die:
Just as the conscript gazers, each one knows,
Might parachute upon their gazing foes:
Invaders from a foreign century.
I hear a whisper scratching at my ear—

An ancient hag drew back her lips to breathe
Her ecstasy upon the festive air.
She might well be the oldest woman there
—Or so the concentration in her teeth
And damp absorption in her eyes suggest.

A wisp of gesture spirals from her wrist
Towards the crimson sky. The oldest there?
The sky turns gold. I wonder if for her
Algeria or 'eighty-nine exist.
The fading sparks find mirrors in her eyes.

Who are the fireworks for? Old hags, old men,
Children up late, and straggling foreigners?
No-one is old enough to know the cause,
Or young enough to feel he is not in
A troubled crowd beneath a troubled sky.

SYDNEY CLOUTS

The Hawk

The hawk broods earthward
On glimmering scythes;
Darkens the mountain,
Darkens the field.

A white cloud goes over—
So pure, I cry out
For a word of judgement.
The shadow drops down.

The flowers are toppling,
The earth burbles blood.
O scholars of Mercy,
Interpret the flood!

SYDNEY CLOUTS

The Sleeper

(For Marge)

When you awake
Gesture will waken
To decisive things.
Asleep, you have taken
Motion and tenderly laid it
Within, deeply within you.
Your shoulders are shining
With your own clear light.
I should be mistaken
To touch you even softly,
To disturb your bold
And entirely personal devotion
To the self that sleeps,
And is your very self,
Crucial as when you hasten
In the house and hasten through the street,
Or sit in the deep yellow chair
And breathe sweet air.

Unaware of the stars
Outside your window
That do not know they shine;
As well as of the wild sea
That can have no care;
As well as of the wind
That blows unaware
Of its motion in the air,
Sound be your rest
And gentle the dreaming
Of your silent body
Passionately asleep.
Can a cloud stay so still?
Can a bird be so lonely?
It seems you have found
Great patience in your breath:
It moves with life,
It rehearses death.

SYDNEY CLOUTS

Of Thomas Traherne and the Pebble Outside

Gusts of the sun race on the approaching sea.
In the air Traherne's brightness shines.
A jewelled Garden gazed at him.
What shall be said of Paradise?
Fused space and fire store the hard pebble I hold.
The long rock-sheltered surges flash with spume.
I have read firm poems of God.
Good friend, you perceived bright angels.
This heathen bit of the world lies warm in my palm.

SYDNEY CLOUTS

Within

You look long about you,
Intent on the world
On a midsummer day.
But the sea flames hard,
It is rumpled like tin,
The sun is burning
Dimension away.
If you cast a pebble down
It will clatter on the waves;
Your eye can not go in.
And it cannot find a tree
Standing generous and full,
Or a house or flower
With individual power.
And it must not look within—
Hardness afflicts you,
Flat is the world you'd find:
A row of wooden rooftops
That can easily topple
And can bring the heart down,
And bring down the mind.

SYDNEY CLOUTS

The Sea and the Eagle

The sea contains a destiny,
Also the broadwinged eagle.
Both with an equal loneliness
Devour their continents.

Bird, where are you bound,
Borne on the surfs of height?
There is nothing unknown in the air.
Why do your wings flow up and upward?

Whose silence, waters, and what wound
Do you conceal in thunder?
Your beak has worried the bones of earth
Longer than the seasons have been about
Our robes, rising and falling,
And mingling us in the flowing metre.

We have given you both a mystery.
Reveal it and we shall see ourselves
Suddenly like a rising wing,
Terribly like a swoop of water.

SYDNEY CLOUTS

Roy Kloof

'Such a little king's eye,' said my mother,
Who still had the kind imperial look.
'He'll command. Dear cherry-bright boy!'
Her faded English blood ran strong;
She dreamt of the shires all night long,
Rose in the morning and called me Roy.

That was the beginning. My father who came
Raw from the veld with a rocky name,
Though a mild man, frequently dreamt
That Circumstance galloped with him riding,
That History was thatched into his roof.
It hurt him to hear me christened, Roy Kloof.

Up behind father with little bright spurs
I dreamt I was galloping, gravely horsed.
I dreamt of a sceptre; I cried and I cried,
Till rock and shire were divorced.
Division incarnate! An unhappy role!
My country has given me flint for a soul.

SYDNEY CLOUTS

Roy Kloof went Riding

Near a field overflowing
With barley, I ride.

My mother embroiders
And lives by the sea.
Small money she makes,
With shimmering tones
Of a tower on top of a distant hill,
And combs of water hard and still,
And sprinkled cherries made
The size of blood.

On Sundays I visit
My father; he greets me
With sombre surprise.
And sometimes and terribly
Laughs with such pain,
That his stubbled morgen
Carry the sound from stone to stone,
Then strike it through my marrowbone.
His second wife restored
His faith in God.

I have a small house
And a gentle child,
A young wife's care
And a good field.
The season of berries
And vines I love;
But the hill I climb has a heavy tree
That surges with quarrels, and darkens me
To a desperate mind that throws
Torn light as it blows.

SYDNEY CLOUTS

The Situation

Red mountain, red forest.
Of curious quiet, the late afternoon.
Politics hangs a long hand over the wall.
Is the sun setting, is it the sun?
This chocolate sweetens thought.
When the dung-beetle scratches, the noise echoes in the house.
Come wind, blow wind blow!
I stand still in my garden.
Let us elect a Minister from some wise stones.
Set the wine on the table.
Dead thought is swarming with tyrannical flies.
The clouds are in congress.
Set down the fruit.
Of exultant serenity shine the firm plums.
Cleft rocks, torn fish in the sea.

WILLIAM BRANFORD

Trooper Temple Pulvermacher

(*Killed in action, Mount Hope, Cape Province, 26 October 1901*)

I

Forgotten soldier, in the winter grass,
Still ambushed for my step, among the rocks
And creviced hills that looked upon your death,
In the reconnaissance of the hare, the mica-fleck's
Miniature helio, and the entanglements
Of thorn and sugarbush, your human stealth,

Capacity for skirmish and attack,
Seem to survive, and fascinate as if
Perpetuating you.
And in the life of beasts and vegetation,
Here, in the valley of your last day's fighting,
Strange echoes of the sterile skills of war
Almost delight me, bringing you to mind.
And yet you're nothing to me but a word
On a memorial brass, so what's your warrant
For lurking in the memory, except
Unlucky soldiership, spent in a bad quarrel?

II

Well, after fifty years, yours is an easy death
To come to terms with, as the morning's breath
Flatters the lungs, and the Long Kloof extends
A boundless country of imagined friends.
When, like a shadow or a light unsought
You come to darken or inflame my thought,
Is not narcotic pity free to dote
On agonies conveniently remote,
Or idle intellect to contemplate
Hypotheses to justify your fate?
No surer provocation it's been said
For loose emotion than the anonymous dead.

III

Morning marches into the valley, overwhelming
The strong-points of the mist; unseen
Creatures of half-light, forsaking the haunts of man,
Withdraw to the pathless hills.
But you, invisible inhabitant
Of thought, hold out against the thrusting sunlight.

For death is more than the rifleman's misjudgement,
More than whatever material accident,
Choice of wrong cover or failure of vigilance
Brought upon you.
Death itself is your claim to compassion.
Illusions vanish with dew, but no evaporation
Of private fiction, sentimental detail,
Breaks down the substance of your right to memory.

And I see you as guardian, sentinel over
Life's secret frontier, because you lie
Here, remote from political priestcraft
And synthetic humanism. For here indifferent rock,
Cactus and thornbush forbid irresponsible
Funeral oration, tolerant only
Of reticent sympathy:
The root's comprehension of earth, or the combatant aloe's
Grasp of essentials.

PETER JACKSON

In Loco

This afternoon I take the path alone
That scales knowingly the mammoth kopje
To the cavern in its flank, and find
The small beast hanging rank upon the air,
Dung of the rock-rabbit, no sovereigns:
Or quill of porcupine, dropped where he wrote
Abandoned. No shade springs up to brandish
The broken assegai and half-buried spear.

Stupid, to send despair over these hills
Echoing, or raging with a stick
At the adaptable, the spiked and spined,
To milk the innocent cactus in despite;
Which dreams, perhaps, within
The method of its cells, of perilous dark flowers:
Stupid, to ask an echo and a shade
Out of this time with no known precedence.

To us, as a throwing of bones, each day
Hopes to divine the witch of our unease:
The dark roots delving into rock
And fingers folding on the hoard of gold.
A cloud takes up the sun. The watch on my wrist
Tells me where I am, presumes to point
The precise place of being on this hill,
Fixed like a monolith, like making history.

PETER JACKSON

Afrikaans Homestead

Prayers in the whitewashed sitting-room:
An intense ritual, that belies
The heady growth translated to the Cape.
The hair white and the hands scrubbed white.
Fingers like candles lit before the face,
The last years of ambition burning down.

Her eyes, as quick as mice, that missed
Nothing, the cunning scraps and crumbs

Hoarded against the mate she knew would falter,
Never failed her. So she built
Her private offering to the golden goddess:
Against the generations of despite
Became a fountain-head of good achievement,
The matured wine she was now free to sip.

Being her guests, it was enough
We should excuse ourselves, and walk
Jealously among the fields we never worshipped,
To where the indigenous sad eyes
Along the fallen lines were reaping
Another harvest than the hands:
Perhaps the final vintage of a dream.

PETER JACKSON

At the Grave of Cecil Rhodes

Engrossed, the abandoned crickets sing:
One hears it so, termed so,
That high electric monotone, a song.
But the unflowing river silent
The rovambira[1] gliding silent.

Standing upon World's View,
Venus for Mars tonight exchanged,
I think of that late island long ago:
And what, if I dare, atlantic urge
Visited visions on him once,
Set chivalry to search.

[1] Rovambira: a rock-snake.

The crickets utter it, I echo:
Mere tilting for the soul's sake.
'I seek, by day, by night,
Under Venus, under Mars,
A hound, a bay horse and a turtle dove.'

As love is only in the lack of it,
The silent bedrock, the serpent stealing,
The mechanical insect trill:
And the long landscape offering the same,
That damned fatality, an eye-lit world.

PETER JACKSON

Great Zimbabwe

The tributary wish, to be a part,
As birds are famous in the lives of trees:
To the biography of shade each adds a note.

But to be sun in this meridian,
By night the excelling moon.

                    The moon, tonight,
Cool lily in a pool, opens above Zimbabwe,
This valley of a shadow of a shade.

A queen of history, they say, may once
Have taken hence the settings for her jewels
To make an age of gold. Now owl and shrew
Conjoin their little lives to make a night:
The moon exploits a chapter of the story.

Traveller, the moon over Zimbabwe
Proffers no echo from the Parthenon
To soothe your subtlest sensibility:
Disgruntled, your safari takes the dust
And leaves us standing where the ancient road
Runs to Sofala, reads like a river of sand
The ruin of cities paced along its banks,
A tributary road to a queen's heart.

                Tonight, the moon,
A queen in transit, showers upon Zimbabwe
Light of her brightness, silver of her ash.

PETER JACKSON

Dombashawa[1]

And now we climb this bare eroded hill
Where lichens promise meadows, silver grooves
In the smooth granite echo streams gone dry
And the disparate winds of this naked
Morning crack the gaze; all that the eye invents
Becomes the total landscape, where we stand
Under the jurisdiction of the sun.

Morning of winds on Dombashawa hill,
This also can corrupt. Until we see
Time's origin in man, until we hear
Voices of winds deriving from our voice:

[1] Dombashawa Hill, famous for its rock paintings, and ghosts.

A gesture of this summit that creates,
An utterance as primal here as speech,
The discovery of all Africa defined.

But then the caves: these sibylline sad archives
So accurately achieved, the zenith of a school
Flowering where love in symbols of flowers
Never prospered, where truth was sorcery.
Can we still fear these once impassioned texts,
Their auguries locked now in a memory
Of worn stone, the very hill a myth?

It may be late. The few who witness here
The daily brutalizing of our lives
Move to their last migrations. The way of time
Is exigency eating at the legend
Of our love and truth: not the old mysteries
Make fear, but to the still discovering mind
The simple penance of such words brought home.

SOURCES OF THE POEMS

THOMAS PRINGLE: *pp.* 1-7. 'The Emigrants', 'Afar in the Desert', and 'The Desolate Valley' from *The Poetical Works of Thomas Pringle*, Edward Moxon, London, 1837.

CHARLES BARTER: *pp.* 7-12. 'Dingaan and Retief' and 'Changes' from *Stray Memories of Natal and Zululand*, Munro Bros., Printers, Pietermaritzburg, 1897.

RUDYARD KIPLING: *pp.* 13-16. 'Bridge-Guard in the Karroo: 1901' and 'The Burial: 1902' from *The Five Nations*, Methuen & Co., London, 1903.

A. M. BUCKTON: *pp.* 17-20. 'At the Garden Rail' and 'At Welbedacht' from *The Burden of Engela*, Methuen & Co., London, 1904.

A. S. CRIPPS: *pp.* 20-23. 'Resurgat', 'A Pagan's Baptism', 'Lazarus' and 'The Black Christ' from *Africa: Verses*, Oxford University Press, London, 1939.

F. C. SLATER: *pp.* 23-26. 'Lament for a Dead Cow', 'The Wood-Gatherers' and 'Milking Kraal' from *Collected Poems*, William Blackwood & Sons, Edinburgh, 1957.

PERCEVAL GIBBON: *pp.* 26-27. 'Jim' from *A Treasury of South African Poetry and Verse* (ed. Edward Heath Crouch), The Walter Scott Publishing Co., Ltd., London, 1907.

CULLEN GOULDSBURY: *pp.* 28-29. 'The Councillor' from *From the Outposts*, T. Fisher Unwin, London, 1914.

KINGSLEY FAIRBRIDGE: *pp.* 29-30. 'The Song-Maker' from *Fifty Years of Rhodesian Verse* (ed. John Snelling), B. H. Blackwell Ltd., Oxford, 1938, 1939.

BRIAN BROOKE; *pp.* 31-33. 'Smoke of the Camp Fire' from *Poems*, The Bodley Head, London, 1918.

ROY CAMPBELL: *pp.* 33-53. 'Luis de Camoes' from *Talking Bronco*, Faber and Faber Ltd., London, 1946, *from* 'The Flaming Terrapin', 'The Serf', 'The Zulu Girl', 'The Zebras', *from* 'The

Roy Campbell—*cont.*

Wayzgoose', 'On Some South African Novelists', 'On the Same', *from* 'A Veld Eclogue: The Pioneers', 'Rounding the Cape', 'The Sling' and 'Dreaming Spires' from *The Collected Poems of Roy Campbell*, The Bodley Head, London, 1949.

William Plomer: *pp.* 53-67. 'The Death of a Zulu', 'The Pioneers', 'The Explorer' and 'The Victoria Falls' from *Notes for Poems*, The Hogarth Press, London, 1927. 'The Ruined Farm' and 'The Boer War' from *The Fivefold Screen*, The Hogarth Press, London, 1932. 'The Devil-Dancers' from *Visiting the Caves*, Jonathan Cape, London, 1936. 'The Scorpion', 'Namaqualand after Rain', 'Johannesburg' and 'A Traveller's Tale' from *Selected Poems*, The Hogarth Press, London, 1940. 'A Transvaal Morning' from *New Statesman*, 6 October 1956.

Alan Paton: *pp.* 67-72. 'To a Small Boy who Died at Diepkloof Reformatory' from *Towards the Sun* (ed. Macnab), Collins, London, 1950. 'Sanna', 'The Discardment', and 'Samuel', all unpublished.

H. C. Bosman: *pp.* 72-76. 'The Poet', 'Seed', *from* 'The Luck in the Square Stone' and 'Recovery from Mental Illness', all unpublished.

R. N. Currey: *pp.* 76-85. 'Man's Roots', *from* 'Ultimate Exile' and 'Song' from *This Other Planet*, Routledge, London, 1947. 'Marshal Lyautey', 'Morocco' from *Search for Morocco*, unpublished. 'Landscape' from *Indian Landscape*, Routledge, London, 1947. 'Durban Revisited' from *Poetry Commonwealth: Winter 1948-49*, London. 'In Memoriam: Roy Campbell' from *The Listener*, 23 May 1957.

N. H. Brettell: *pp.* 85-91. *From* 'Wind and an Eagle Owl', 'Elephant', 'Giraffes', 'Outside Kimberley' and 'Cataclysm' from *A Rhodesian Leave*, privately published.

Adèle Naudé: *pp.* 91-94. 'The Oracle of Delphi' and 'Memling's Virgin with Apple' from *No Longer at Ease*, A. A. Balkema, Cape Town, 1956.

Margaret Allonby: *pp.* 94-101. 'A Book for Christmas', *from* 'Lustration of the Winter Tree', 'O Theophilus', 'For Sheila', 'Eurydice' and 'Reflection', all unpublished.

CHARLES MADGE: *pp.* 102-106. *From* 'The Hours of the Planets' and 'Delusions VIII' from *The Disappearing Castle*, Faber and Faber Ltd., London, 1937. *From* 'Poem by Stages', unpublished.

F. T. PRINCE: *pp.* 106-115. 'In a Province', 'False Bay' and 'Chaka' from *Poems*, Faber and Faber Ltd., London, 1938. 'The Babiaantje' from *Soldiers Bathing*, The Fortune Press, London, 1954.

ROY FULLER: *pp.* 115-120. 'The Green Hills of Africa', 'The Plains', 'The Tribes' and 'In Africa' from *A Lost Season*, The Hogarth Press, London, 1944.

TERENCE HEYWOOD: *pp.* 120-124. 'Cactus' from *English*. 'Mantis' from *Encounter*, London. 'A Flamingo's Egg' and 'Grisaille' from *Poetry*, Chicago. 'By an Ant-Heap' from *Trails*, U.S.A.

ANTHONY DELIUS: *pp.* 124-136. 'The Coming' from *An Unknown Border*, A. A. Balkema, Cape Town, 1954. From 'The Great Divide' from *Africa South*, *Vol. 1*, *No. 4*, September 1957. 'Chameleon', 'The Gamblers', 'The Explorer' and 'The Pilgrims', all unpublished.

CHARLES EGLINGTON: *pp.* 136-140. 'Cheetah', 'The Vanquished', 'Meeting' and 'Arrival and Departure', all unpublished.

GUY BUTLER: *pp.* 140-151. 'Cape Coloured Batman' and 'Stranger to Europe' from *Stranger to Europe*, A. A. Balkema, Cape Town, 1952. 'Home Thoughts' from *Africa South*, *Vol. 1*, *No. 1*, September 1956. 'David' from *South African PEN Year Book*, C.N.A. Johannesburg, 1957. 'Myths' from *Poets in South Africa* (ed. Macnab), Maskew Miller, Cape Town, 1958. 'Pieta', unpublished.

RUTH MILLER: *pp.* 152-155. 'The Floating Island' from *New Statesman*, December 1957. 'Fruit' from *Poets in South Africa* (ed. Macnab), Maskew Miller, Cape Town, 1958. 'Honey' and 'Fundisi', unpublished.

DAVID WRIGHT: *pp.* 156-169. 'Seven South African Poems' from *Moral Stories*, Derek Verschoyle, London, 1954. 'A Voyage to Africa' from *Monologue of a Deaf Man*, Andre Deutsch, London, 1958.

JOHN PETER: *pp.* 169-174. 'Reading Tolstoy', 'Cypress', 'Christmas on Three Continents', 'Estrangement' and 'Heart's Desire', all unpublished.

Anne Welsh: *pp.* 175-179. 'Sight' from *Standpunte, Vol. 10, No. 6,* June–July 1956. 'Victoria Dancing' and 'The Body's Eye' from *Uneven World,* Hand and Flower Press, London, 1958.

Roy Macnab: *pp.* 179-186. 'Child of the Long Grass' from *Towards the Sun* (ed. Macnab), Collins, London, 1950. 'Majuba Hill' from *Standpunte, Vol. 7, No. 7,* October 1952. *From* 'The Man of Grass' from *Standpunte, Vol. 8, No. 1,* September 1953. 'The Settler' from *South African PEN Year Book,* C.N.A. Johannesburg, 1957.

L. D. Lerner: *pp.* 187-191. 'Senchi Ferry: Gold Coast' from *West Africa.* '14 July 1956' from *New Statesman.* 'The Desert Travellers', unpublished.

Sydney Clouts: *pp.* 191-198. 'Within' from *Standpunte, Vol. 11, No. 1,* September 1956. 'The Sleeper' from *Standpunte, Vol. 11, No. 4,* April 1957. 'The Hawk', 'Of Thomas Traherne and the Pebble Outside', 'The Sea and the Eagle', 'Roy Kloof', 'Roy Kloof went Riding' and 'The Situation', all unpublished.

William Branford: *pp.* 198-200. 'Trooper Temple Pulvermacher', unpublished.

Peter Jackson: *pp.* 200-205. 'In Loco' and 'Great Zimbabwe' from *The London Magazine,* January 1955. 'Afrikaans Homestead' and 'At the Grave of Cecil Rhodes' from *The London Magazine,* March 1956. 'Dombashawa' from *The London Magazine,* February 1957.

BIOGRAPHICAL NOTES

ALLONBY, Margaret

Born on a farm in Orange Free State; early years spent there and in Cumberland; educated at Eunice, Bloemfontein, and the University of the Witwatersrand, where she lectured for a time; member of St. Anne's College, Oxford.

BARTER, Charles

Born 1820. Father Rector of Sarsden, Oxfordshire. Educated at Winchester and New College. Having experienced the 'hardships of a New Brunswick Labour Camp and traversed Canada from East to West', he came to Natal on the *Globe* in 1850, where he eventually settled down as a farmer. Resigned his fellowship of New College on his marriage in 1853. Elective member of the Legislative Council and Magistrate. Died 1904.

Publications:

> *The Dorp and the Veld,* William S. Orr & Co., London, 1852.
> *Stray Memoirs of Natal and Zululand,* Munro Brothers, Pietermaritzburg, 1897.

BOSMAN, Herman Charles

Born Kuils River, Cape Province, 1905. Educated Jeppe Boys' High School, the University of the Witwatersrand and the Normal College; taught in Groot Marico district. Spent four and a half years in prison for shooting his stepbrother. Wrote as a journalist in Johannesburg, London, Brussels, Paris. Died of a heart attack in 1951.

Publications:

Verse
> *The Blue Princess.*
> *Jesus.*

BOSMAN, Herman Charles—*cont.*
Mara
All privately published.

Prose
Jacaranda in the Night, A.P.B., Johannesburg, 1947.
Mafeking Road, C.N.A., Johannesburg, 1947.
Cold Stone Jug, A.P.B., Johannesburg, 1949.

BRANFORD, William
Born, 1927, Southampton, England; educated St. Andrew's College, Grahamstown; St. John's College, Cambridge, and University of Cape Town. Lecturer in English, Natal University, Durban.
Publications:
Poems and articles in various periodicals.
Produced an authorized stage version of Peter Abraham's novel, *Mine Boy*.

BRETTELL, N. H.
Born 1908 at Lye, Worcestershire. Educated at King Edward's Grammar School, Stourbridge, and Birmingham University English School under Ernest de Selincourt. Since 1934 has taught in Southern Rhodesia 'in as remote a part as I can find'.
Publications:
Bronze Frieze, Oxford University Press, 1950.
A Rhodesian Leave, privately published.

BROOKE, Brian
Born Aberdeenshire, 1889; educated Clifton, Gordon's College and Aberdeen University. Emigrated to British East Africa at the age of eighteen; at twenty went tea-planting in Ceylon, but soon returned to Africa, and settled in Uganda. Volunteered on outbreak of war. Died of wounds in France, 1917.
Publications:
Poems, The Bodley Head, London, 1918.

BUCKTON, A. M.
Born 1867. Educated at home at Haslemere. As a young girl she read her poems to Tennyson. Her play, *Eager Heart*, one of the first imitations of the old moralities, attracted some attention, but her poetry did not. She never visited South Africa. Died 1944.

Publications:

    The Burden of Engela, Methuen & Co., London, 1904.

    Eager Heart, Methuen & Co., London, 1951 (latest edition).

    Kings in Babylon, Methuen & Co., 1906.

    Songs of Joy, Methuen & Co., 1908.

    A Catechism of Life, Methuen & Co., 1912.

    Daybreak and Other Poems, Methuen & Co., 1918.

BUTLER, Guy
Born at Cradock, Cape Province, 1918. Educated at local High School; Rhodes University, Grahamstown, and Brasenose College, Oxford. War service in Middle East, Italy and United Kingdom, 1940–5. English Editor of *Standpunte* since 1956. Professor of English, Rhodes University. Two plays performed by S.A. National Theatre Organization.

Publications:

  Verse

    Stranger to Europe, Balkema, Cape Town, 1952.

  Plays

    The Dam, Balkema, Cape Town, 1953.

    The Dove Returns, Fortune Press, London, 1956.

CAMPBELL, Roy
Born in Durban, 1901; educated Durban High School; to Oxford for one year in 1920; lived in Spain, France and Portugal, with brief periods in Great Britain, and three visits to South Africa; 1926, edited *Voorslag* with William Plomer. Wounded fighting for Franco in Spain, and in Second World War. Service in East Africa and Western Desert. Discharged, 1944, and joined B.B.C. 1952. Killed in a car accident in Portugal, 1957.

CAMPBELL, Roy—*cont.*

Publications:

Verse

The Flaming Terrapin, Cape, 1924.

The Wayzgoose, Cape, 1928.

Adamastor, Faber, 1930.

The Georgiad, Boriswood, 1931.

Flowering Reeds, Boriswood, 1933.

Mithraic Emblems, Boriswood, 1936.

Flowering Rifle, Longmans, 1939.

Talking Bronco, Faber, 1946.

Translations

St. John of the Cross, Harvill Press, 1951.

Baudelaire, Harvill Press, 1952.

Autobiographies

Broken Record, Boriswood, 1934.

Light on a Dark Horse, Hollis and Carter, 1951.

CLOUTS, Sydney

Born in Cape Town, 1926; educated University of Cape Town.

CRIPPS, Arthur Searly

Born in Tunbridge Wells, 1869; educated Charterhouse and Trinity College, Oxford. Boxing Blue. Ordained, 1892. To Mashonaland in 1907, where he lived among the tribesmen as a missionary until his death in 1952.

Publications:

Primavera (with Laurence Binyon, Stephen Phillips and Manhomon Chase), 1890.

The Black Christ, Blackwell, 1902.

Lyra Evangelistica, Blackwell, 1909.

African Verses, Oxford University Press, 1939.

CURREY, Ralph Nixon

Born Mafeking, 1907; educated Ermelo, Transvaal; Kingswood School, Bath; and Wadham College, Oxford. Served in Royal

CURREY, Ralph Nixon—*cont.*

Artillery during the war. Now Senior English Master at Colchester Royal Grammar School. Broadcasts for B.B.C.

Publications:

> *Tiresias*, Oxford University Press, 1940.
>
> *This Other Planet*, Routledge, 1945.
>
> Ed., with Gibson, *Poems from India* (Forces Anthology), Oxford University Press, 1945.
>
> *Indian Landscape*, Routledge, 1947.
>
> *Formal Spring* (Translations of Renaissance French Poetry), Oxford University Press, 1950.
>
> *Between Two Worlds*, Dramatic Poem for Radio. B.B.C., Third Programme.

DELIUS, Anthony

Born Simonstown, 1916; part of childhood on Transvaal farm; educated St. Aidan's College and Rhodes University (B.A.), Grahamstown. Served in Intelligence Corps; after the war joined *Saturday Post*, Port Elizabeth, and then became Parliamentary Correspondent and leader writer on *Cape Times*. English editor of *Standpunte* till 1956.

Publications:

> Verse
>
> > *An Unknown Border*, Balkema, Cape Town, 1954.
>
> Travel
>
> > *A Young Traveller in South Africa*, Phoenix House, London, 1947.
> >
> > *The Long Way*, Howard Timmins, Cape Town, 1956.

EGLINGTON, Charles

Born in Johannesburg, 1918, and grew up in the Western Province, where his father was a farmer; educated at the Franschhoek School, the Diocesan College, Rondebosch, and the University of the Witwatersrand, Johannesburg. Served with the Union's forces in North Africa and Italy, 1940–5. Feature writer and book reviewer on the staff of *The Friend* in Bloemfontein.

FAIRBRIDGE, Kingsley

Born in Grahamstown, C.P., 1885, where he went to school at

FAIRBRIDGE, Kingsley—*cont.*

St. Andrew's College. Family emigrated to Umtali, Rhodesia in 1896. First Rhodes Scholar, 1908, Exeter College, Oxford. Founder of the Child Immigration Society. Died 1924.

Publications:

    Veld Verse, Oxford University Press, 1928.

    Autobiography, Oxford University Press, 1934.

FULLER, Roy

Born, England, 1912. Served Royal Navy, 1941–6. In Africa, 1942–3, mainly at Royal Navy Air Station, Nairobi, but also at Tanga, Durban, and Cape Town. A solicitor.

Publications:

    Six books of verse; one of which—*A Lost Season* (The Hogarth Press, London, 1944)—almost wholly on African themes.

    Savage Gold, one of his books for children, has an African setting.

    Novels—three, the most recent being *Image of a Society*.

GIBBON, Perceval

Born in Wales, 1879, and educated in Germany; joined *Rand Daily Mail* in 1902, but returned to United Kingdom after a few years. Wrote three novels and one book of poems. Died 1926.

Publications:

  Verse

    African Items, Elliot Stock, London, 1903.

  Novels

    Souls in Bondage, Blackwood, London, 1904.

    Salvator, Blackwood, London, 1908.

    Margaret Harding, Blackwood, London, 1911.

GOULDSBURY, Cullen

Born 1881. Son of an officer in the Indian Police; joined the British South African Company in 1902, where he served first in Native Administration and then as a District Officer in Northern Rhodesia. Joined King's African Rifles in 1914. Died at Tanga, East Africa, 1916.

GOULDSBURY, Cullen—*cont.*

Publications:

    Rhodesian Rhymes, Philpott and Collins, Bulawayo, 1909.
    Songs out of Exile, T. Fisher Unwin, London, 1912.
    From the Outposts, T. Fisher Unwin, London, 1914.

HEYWOOD, Terence
Born Johannesburg, of New Zealand parents; educated P.T.P.S.,
Johannesburg; Malvern College; Worcester College, Oxford (M.A.),
and a short period at Uppsala University, Sweden. Since the age of
fourteen visits to South Africa infrequent. Has been a free-lance
writer, and also engaged in Forestry. At present with Association of
Special Libraries and Information Bureaux.

Publications:

  Verse

    How Smoke Gets into the Air, Fortune Press, 1951.
    Architectonic, Fortune Press, 1953.

  Travel

    Background to Sweden, Constable, 1951.
    Facing North (with Dr. Edward Lowbury), Mitre Press, London,
    1958.

JACKSON, Peter
Born Yorkshire, 1928. Read English at New College, Oxford. 1951,
Southern Rhodesian Native Affairs Department; 1956, Executive
Officer of Capricorn Africa Society, Northern Rhodesia. Poems in
London Magazine.

KIPLING, Rudyard
Born Bombay, 1865; educated United Services College, Westward
Ho. First visited the Cape in 1891, second journey 1898. From 1900
to 1908 the family visited South Africa every year. Most of his South
African verse appeared in *The Five Nations*, 1903. Died, 1936.

Publications:

    Prolific writer in verse (*Departmental Ditties*, 1886, *Barrack Room
    Ballads*, 1892, etc.) and prose (*Plain Tales from the Hills*, 1888.
    The Jungle Book, 1894, *Stalky & Co.*, 1899, *Kim*, 1901, &c.)

LERNER, L. D.
Born Cape Town, 1925. University of Cape Town, 1942–5; and entered Pembroke College, Cambridge, 1947. Lecturer in English at the University College of the Gold Coast, 1949–53; now extra-mural lecturer at the Queen's University of Belfast. Poems and criticism have appeared in various periodicals.

MACNAB, Roy
Born Durban, 1923; educated Hilton and Jesus College, Oxford. War Service with Royal Navy. Reporter on Staff of *Natal Daily News*; at present Cultural Attaché, South Africa House, London.
Publications:

> *Testament of a South African*, Fortune Press, 1947.
> Co-editor, *Oxford Poetry*, 1947, Blackwell, and *South African Poetry, a New Anthology*, Collins, 1948.
> Ed. *Towards the Sun*, Collins, London, 1950.
> Ed. *Poets in South Africa*, Maskew Miller, Cape Town, 1958.

MADGE, Charles
Born Johannesburg, 1912; educated Winchester and Cambridge. Co-founder of Mass-Observation in 1937. Appointed Professor of Social Science, University of Birmingham, in 1950.
Publications:

> Verse
>
>> *The Disappearing Castle*, Faber, 1937.
>> *The Father Found*, Faber, 1941.

MILLER, Ruth
Born at Uitenhage, Cape Province, 1919; educated at St. Pius' Convent, Pietersburg, Transvaal. Poems published in *South African Opinion*, *London Magazine*, etc.

NAUDÉ, Adèle
Born Pretoria, 1910; educated at Rustenburg Girls' High School, Cape Town, and the University of Cape Town (B.A.). Has been Academic Assistant to Registrar, University of Cape Town, secretary, freelance journalist in both official languages.

NAUDÉ, Adèle—*cont.*

Publications:

Verse

No Longer at Ease, Balkema, Cape Town, 1956.

Afrikaans poems in periodicals.

Prose

Children's books in Afrikaans.

PATON, Alan

Born Pietermaritzburg, Natal, 1903; educated at Maritzburg College and University of Natal (B.Sc., B.Ed.). Taught in Natal schools for eleven years; in 1935 appointed Principal of Diepkloof Reformatory near Johannesburg; resigned in 1948 to devote time to writing. An Honorary L.H.D. degree from Yale University in 1954. Elected National Chairman of South African Liberal Party in 1956.

Publications:

Cry the Beloved Country, Cape, 1948.

Too Late the Phalarope, Cape, 1953.

(Both have been translated into most European languages.)

South Africa and Her People, Lutterworth Press, 1955.

South Africa in Transition, Scribners, New York, 1956.

PETER, John

Born 1921 at Queenstown, Cape Province; educated there, Rhodes University, and Gonville and Caius College, Cambridge. For the past seven years has lived in Canada, where he is Professor of English in the University of Manitoba, visiting South Africa for a year in 1957–8.

Publications:

Complaint and Satire in Early English Literature, Clarendon Press, 1956.

Critical articles, stories and poems in English and American periodicals.

PLOMER, William

Born Pietersburg, N. Transvaal, 1903; educated partly in South Africa (St. John's College, Johannesburg) and partly in England (Rugby). After farming in eastern Cape Province and trading in Zululand, worked with Roy Campbell to produce literary magazine, *Voorslag*, in Natal, 1926. Later lived in Japan and Greece. Settled in England. Served on Naval Staff at Admiralty, 1940–5. Fellow of Royal Society of Literature. Acts as publisher's literary adviser. Visited South Africa in 1956 as guest speaker at a Conference of University Teachers, Publishers and Writers, University of the Witwatersrand, Johannesburg.

Publications:

Five novels from *Turbott Wolfe* (1925) to *Museum Pieces* (1952).

Seven volumes of poems, the most recent being *A Shot in the Park* (1955).

Four volumes of short stories, the first being *I Speak of Africa* (1927).

Lives of Cecil Rhodes and Ali Pasha.

Autobiography: *Double Lives* (1943), *At Home* (1958).

Ed. *Kilvert's Diary, 1870–1879* (3 vols.: 1938–40), and *Curious Relations*, by William d'Arfey, etc.

PRINCE, Frank Templeton

Born Kimberley, Cape Province, 1912; educated Christian Brothers College, Kimberley; Balliol College, Oxford; Graduate College, Princeton, U.S.; Intelligence Corps, 1940–6. Since 1946 Reader in English Literature, University of Southampton.

Publications:

Verse

Poems, Faber, 1938.

Soldiers Bathing, Fortune Press, 1954.

Criticism

The Italian Element in Milton's Verse, Oxford University Press, 1954.

PRINGLE, Thomas

Born Scotland, 1789; educated Edinburgh University. Acquainted with Scott and subsequently Coleridge. Emigrated to South Africa with British Settlers in 1820. After two years on the Frontier he was appointed as Government Librarian, Cape Town. With his friend Fairbairn he established the *South African Journal* (1824). Their stand against the Governor, Lord Charles Somerset, who wished to suppress it, established the freedom of the Press in South Africa. After a further visit to the Frontier, he returned to England in 1826, where he was appointed Secretary to the Anti-Slavery Society. Died, 1834.

Publications:

> *Narrative of a Residence in South Africa*, Edward Moxon, London, 1835.
> *The Poetical Works of Thomas Pringle*, Edward Moxon, London, 1837.

SLATER, Francis Carey

Born Alice, Cape Province, 1876; educated at Lovedale (then a mixed school for Europeans and Africans). From 1899 to his retirement he served in banks in various towns in the Eastern Cape. Died, 1958.

Selected Publications:

> *Footpaths through the Veld*, Blackwood, 1905.
> *From Mimosa Land*, Blackwood, 1910.
> *The Karroo*, Blackwood, 1924.
> *A Centenary Book of South African Verse*, Longmans, 1925.
> *Drought*, Benn, 1929.
> *Dark Folk*, Blackwood, 1935.
> *Collected Poems*, Blackwood, 1957.

WELSH, Anne

Born Johannesburg, 1922; educated Kingsmead School, Johannesburg, and Roedean, Brighton; University of the Witwatersrand, Johannesburg, and Somerville College, Oxford. Lecturer in Economics, University of the Witwatersrand.

Publication:

> *Uneven World: Poems*, Hand and Flower Press, 1958.

WRIGHT, David

Born Johannesburg, 1920. Left South Africa in 1934, since when he has visited it twice, in 1936 and 1951. Educated Northampton School for the Deaf, and Oriel College, Oxford. In 1950 he received an Atlantic Award for Literature of £250.

Publications:

    Poems, Editions Poetry, London, 1949.

    Moral Stories, Verschoyle, London, 1954.

    Ed., with John Heath-Stubbs, *The Forsaken Garden*, Lehmann, 1950: *The Faber Book of Twentieth Century Verse*, Faber, 1953.

    Beowulf, a prose translation, Penguin Classics, 1957.

    Monologue of a Deaf Man, Deutsch, London, 1958.

INDEX OF AUTHORS

INDEX OF TITLES AND FIRST LINES

Titles in *italic* type; first lines in roman

224

226